NOW LISTEN, WARDEN

NOW LISTEN,
WARDEN

BY RAY P. HOLLAND

ILLUSTRATED BY WESLEY DENNIS

COACHWHIP PUBLICATIONS

Greenville, Ohio

Now Listen, Warden, by Ray P. Holland
First published 1946.
Raymond Prunty Holland (1884-1973).
© 2013 Coachwhip Publications
No claim made on public domain material.

ISBN 1-61646-185-3
ISBN-13 978-1-61646-185-0

CoachwhipBooks.com

*This book is dedicated
to my many friends throughout the country
whose job in life is game protection, and
to those other friends who must have a game
warden to look after them when they go
afield with either rod or gun.*

CONTENTS

FOREWORD

THIS is a book of game warden yarns. Some of them are old—very old. But then, only good stories live to a ripe old age. Some of these yarns are true, most of them have a foundation of truth. A good story retold seldom loses in the telling.

In the early years of game management in this country, the game warden was seldom a man to be looked up to in the community. Rather he was the village loafer who could swing a few votes at election time. He usually liked to hunt and fish, but as an enforcement officer he just didn't rate. Today, in most sections, this has changed. In many states, sportsmen's organizations have divorced game protection from politics and the game protector is a respected citizen who sees to it that the laws are observed and the game is played fairly.

FOREWORD

I have known all types of game wardens from barflies to the college-trained game-management experts. When the Federal Government took on the job of protecting migratory birds, I was one of the first District Inspectors, with a number of Western states to look after. Since man knoweth not to the contrary I have been Secretary-Treasurer of the International Association of Game, Fish and Conservation Commissioners. Also, I have held and still hold office in local and national sportsmen's organizations. With that background, I believe I have heard more game warden yarns than any man alive.

In the annals of game conservation there are many stories filled with drama and suspense. I once arrested the Attorney-General of the state of Missouri—and convicted him of shooting ducks in the spring of the year in violation of Federal law. The ramifications of that case would make a book in itself. It's a good yarn, and that arrest resulted in the Supreme Court decision which decided the constitutionality of the Federal law protecting migratory birds But it is not for this book.

Then there was the case of the New York game and poultry dealer who took out a game-breeding license and had his up-state game farm. His trappers caught birds alive and shipped them to the farm. There they were killed and sent to market. It took some clever detective work to unravel this one. If the poultry dealer hadn't started raising in quantity such wild ducks as canvasbacks, which have never been successfully raised in captivity, he would have done right well. As it was, he paid the largest cash fine in game-law history. But that story doesn't belong in a book of this kind.

There was the wealthy fox-hunting club with their red coats and fine horse flesh that rode to hounds twice a week and ate venison between times—said venison being killed on order by the flunkies. Of course, the hounds were bothered by the deer, and occasionally they would leave the fox to chase an old buck, which would spoil the sport. And besides, the deer were good to eat, and who ever heard of eating a fox? These boys and girls dug down pretty deep when they paid the piper, but nothing as sordid as that will be told in detail in this volume.

Instead, these yarns are retold solely for amusement. Many funny things happen to game wardens. Your warden is a law-enforcement officer, but in the main he is not dealing with criminals. His contacts are with fellows who are cheating a little and who never have weighed the chances of getting caught. Most of them lie with utter abandon. This, at times, becomes very humorous, but incidents do occur in the life of a warden that are really funny. It is such stories that you will find in these pages. I only hope my readers will agree with me that these yarns are funny and that they will have as much fun reading, as I had writing, them.

R. P. H.

NOW LISTEN, WARDEN

THE WORLD'S BIGGEST LIAR

THIS first story is the granddaddy of all the game warden yarns. I can't remember back far enough to date it. In fact, as I ponder the matter I am willing to take oath that I have had this story told to me in at least thirty different states, and each teller had his own version. Make no mistake, a finished raconteur will know both the warden and the liar. The chances are better than even that he was right there when the thing happened.

Admitting that good stories, like good wine, improve with age, I still must present this first story with an apology. However, I have one good excuse to include the yarn in a book of this kind. I told it to the editor of one of the country's foremost magazines, and he laughed and claimed he had never heard it. If a man who makes his living reading and sorting other fellows' stories has never heard about the world's biggest liar, there may be others here and there who should be enlightened.

A game warden entered the smoking car on a slow train through Arkansas and seated himself alongside a man whose abundance of sample cases proved him to be a "knight of the grip." Now, traveling men are often unconsciously of great assistance to game wardens by that loquaciousness which ever marks their profession. Therefore, the warden started the ball a-rolling.

4

"Lots o' game in this country, ain't there?"

"Game! Well, I'll tell the world," replied the traveling man, and before the warden could get in another word he was off.

"Tell you what I did last Sunday. I had to lay over at a little place south of here, so I borrowed a gun from a customer and bought an even hundred shells and walked over to a cypress brake for a little mallard shooting. The ducks were so thick in that swamp that any kind of a shot would have been able to run a hundred straight, but darn my soul if I didn't miss my ninety-fourth shot. When I went in, I made up my mind to shoot only greenheads, and I brought out ninety-nine of the scamps. Fat and fine, I'll say they were."

The warden looked past his new acquaintance through the car window for a second or so at a big flock of these same mallards circling a rice-field. Then he remarked, "I am afraid you do not know who I am."

"No, I'm afraid I don't," was the glib reply.

"Well," continued the man charged with the protection of the state's game, "I'm the game warden for this district."

"Hum," meditated this marvelous shot. "I'll just bet you have no idea who I am."

"I assure you I have not that pleasure," answered the warden.

"Well, sir, I'll tell you," said the plush-cushion duck hunter as he began gathering his bags together for the next station. "I'm the biggest damned liar this side of the Mississippi!"

A SMART BOY

IN ORDER to secure a conviction, a warden must have the *prima facie* evidence. He can see a man shoot a duck out of season, but if he can't get his hands on that duck he will have a tough time convincing the killer. In court it would be his word against that of his prisoner,

and no intelligent warden is going to run the risk of being tongue-lashed by the judge for coming before him without a case.

In New York state the season on black bass does not open until the middle of June. Anglers fishing for pickerel or perch often catch many bass which, according to law, must be taken from the hook as gently as possible and returned to the water. It is not hard to believe that many people find this a very difficult task to perform, especially if the perch or pickerel are not striking. The state game protectors are very vigilant, and a small black bass has been the undoing of many a pompous angler.

One spring day, forget the year, a state game protector, probably called plain game warden in those days, stopped beside a young farmer lad who was fishing in a lake near his home. The catch was examined and found to consist of yellow and white perch only. The protector was about to go on, when he heard a fish flouncing around in the water close to shore and some little distance along the bank.

Walking up to investigate, he found about four pounds of smallmouth bass tied securely to an overhanging willow. Here was something that called for action, but as the fish was quite a distance from the fisherman he thought best to walk back and engage the boy in conversation in an effort to make him claim ownership of the illegal fish.

"Any bass in this lake?" was the first question.

"Lots of 'em," was the answer.

"Catch any?" was the next.

"It's ag'in the law this time of year," was the reply.

"Well, then," thundered the protector, "will you explain to me why you strung that four-pound smallmouth and tied him fast? Now, don't lie to me, for I saw you do it, and I have just walked up the shore to see if he was still there. Wait a minute, I'm not through. I want you to understand that I'm the state game protector, and that I've been watching you with field-glasses from across the lake and saw you catch that fish and string it. Now tell me why, and why you didn't return it to the water, as the law provides, and which you admit you know you should have done."

"That's all easy to explain," answered the boy. "You see, it was this way. Ma wanted a mess of perch for supper, and I told her I'd come over to the lake and catch 'em for her. She was powerful set on havin' a good mess 'cause we was goin' to have company.

"Well, no sooner had I throwed my hook in until somethin' stole my worm. I just couldn't keep her baited. A time or two I hooked the thief, but he straightened my little perch hook right out. I knew it was one of them old gluttons; so I put on a bigger hook and a gob of worms and caught him. Now, you see it wouldn't have done me no good to have turned him loose again and had him go on eatin' my bait, so I just strung him and tied him upshore out of the way until I finish fishin' and then I'm goin' to up and turn him loose."

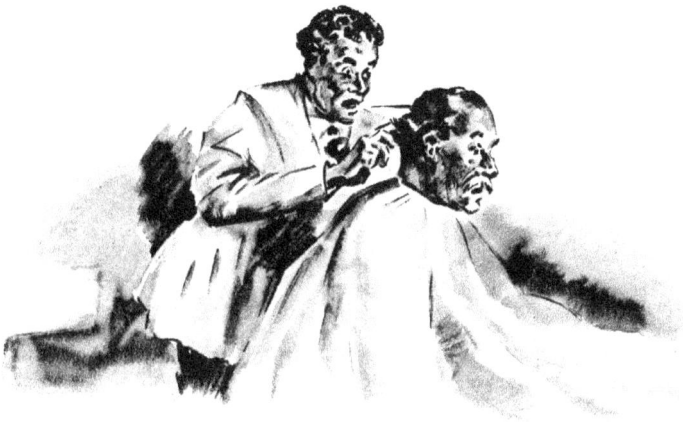

WHO KILLA DA HAIN?

Dominick Di Pippo is my barber. Just because he is of Italian birth and has certain difficulties with our language, do not think he is not a good American. Intimate it to him, and he will show you his final papers and also a medal he won under the Stars and Stripes for marksmanship while at a southern cantonment in World War I.

Dominick is also a good barber, for he talks incessantly. Knowing that I am interested in game and hunting, this topic generally monopolizes the conversation while my hair is being trimmed, for hunting is also a passion with Dominick.

No sooner had I seated myself in the barber's chair on my last visit to his tonsorial parlor than he was off, full speed, with the throttle wide open. "You know Tony Ferrarro and data rabbit dog Lucy?" he asked me, and before I could say "No" he was well in the middle of his story.

"You see, it's disa way. I'm a sport. I no shoota songbird. I shoota game. Deesa wops wot shoota chippy sparrow maka me so dog-gone mad. I talk to dem. It doa no good. I hope da damn game-a-ward geta dem all. Lasta week I see Tony Ferrarro wot owns dat rabbit dog Lucy, and he is talkin' with Garibaldi Guglielmo and Mike Ruggiero. Dosa fellas all shoota chippy sparrow. I go up and tell dem why not be reg'lar sports and not breaka law.

WHO KILLA DA HAIN?

I tell dem on Saturday we can shoota roosta pheasant by
law and dat I taka my Hup and we four geta four roosta
pheasant. Maybe we get dozen roosta pheasant, have
much luck, and maybe some rabs. Dey alla say sure, so
we go.

"Now, Dominick, he gooda sport and no breaka law.
He talk like Dutch uncle to dosa wops. He tell dem w'en
with Dominick dey no breaka any law. Dey musta no
shoot chippy sparrow any color. Dey musta hunt roosta
pheasant and rabs. Dominick tolda dosa wops de musta no
shoota hain pheasant, which against da law. Dominick tell
dem hain brown and roosta have all color; no chance
mistake hain for roosta.

"I stop dat Hup of mine near little swamp, and we go
down edge. Mike he see chippy sparrow, all red breast,
and he wanta shoot. I tell him 'No.' We all gooda sport;
shoot only roosta pheasant and a rab. Data rabbit dog
Lucy, she go out in swamp and soon she say, 'Whoo, woo,
woa, yip.' And I say, 'Looka out, data rabbit dog she runa
roosta pheasant.' We see dat rabbit dog Lucy coma our
way, and we geta ready.

" 'Flap!' Outa grass come big hain pheasant. 'Bang!'

13

goes Tony, and down goes hain pheasant. By goll, I geta mad. I tolda Tony he breaka law. He say he no care. I say no sport breaka law. He say hain pheasant just good to eat as roosta pheasant. I say, by goll, he no touch hain or I tell game-a-ward. Den Tony he geta mad. He just raisa hell. I say go 'head, just touch hain and I tella game-a-ward. He so mad he kick hain. I tell him he touch hain again I tella game ward. He say he eat hain. I say lika hell. Den Tony he geta big mad and he calla his rabbit dog Lucy and he go off hunt by himself.

"Garibaldi, Mike and Dominick, we go on to hunta roosta pheasant and leava hain ona ground. Data afta-noon Tony he find us. He got all over his mad. He say I right, he wrong. No shoota 'notha hain. He have one fina roosta and two rabs. We have one roosta pheasant. We go on geta two more rabs; data rabbit dog Lucy, she gooda dog.

"Data night we coma downa road and we meet a game-a-ward. He know me and say 'Hello, Dominick.'

"I say, 'Hello, Mr. Game-a-Ward.'

"He say, 'Dominick?'

"I say, 'Wot?'

WHO KILLA DA HAIN?

"He say, 'Who killa da hain?'"

"I say, 'Mr. Game-a-Ward, we no killa hain. We alla good sport. We shoota roosta pheasant and a rab,' and I take out roosta with big, longa tail and show da game-a-ward I shoota roosta.

"Dat game-a-ward he looka at me and he say, 'Dominick?'"

"I say, 'Wot?'"

"He say, 'Who killa da hain?'"

"I say, 'Honest to gosh, Mr. Game-a-Ward, we no killa hain. We gooda sport. We all got our lice'. We no hunt until we buy lice'. We no shoota chippy sparrow. You know me, Mr. Game-a-Ward. I no breaka law. I see wop breaka law maka me so goldarn mad I coma tella you.'

"Data game-a-ward, he just stand and look at me and then he say, 'Dominick?'"

"And I say, 'Wot?'"

"And he say, 'Who killa da hain?'"

"I say, 'By goll, Mr. Game-a-Ward, can't you believe me? We no killa hain. We see hain lay dead on da ground and we stan' and look. And we say we no touch; we know it against da law to kill hain and we say some nocounta wop shoota hain. Mike, Garibaldi, Tony and Dominick all say, "Too bad," and we find who killa hain we coma tell you.'

"Data game-a-ward he just standa like a fool and he say, 'Who killa da hain?'

"I say, 'Wotta mat', Mr. Game-a-Ward? Dominick gooda boy; Garibaldi gooda boy; Mike a gooda boy, and Tony too.'

"And then dat game-a-ward he talk a lot. He say he sorry much. He thought I was a gooda citzen. He surprised. He say he hate-a arrest me, but duty was a duty. He no talk at all about arrest dat wop Tony or about my gooda friends Mike or Garibaldi.

"I say, 'Looka here, Mr. Game-a-Ward, wotta mat? I no shoota hain. You know me. I gooda sport. I gooda citzen. I geta decorate in da war.'

"Data game-a-ward he just look at me and I talk and talk and w'en I can no talk more, which was soma time, he justa say, 'Dominick?'

"And I say, 'Wot?'

"And he say, 'Whose car dat down by da little swamp?'

"Now, I'm proud dat Hup and I say, 'Mr. Game-a-

16

Ward, data my car.'

   "And he say, 'Dominick?'

   "And I say, 'Wot?'

   "And he say, 'Unda da back seat in dat car is a dead hain pheasant.'

   "And I say, 'My God!' "

BEER BOTTLE CAPS

Most game-law violations are hard to detect if the law is broken intentionally and the man who breaks it is smart. Catching a fellow shooting without a license, or with one bird more than he should have, or a short fish are all simple enough. It is a different story when you start out to catch a vicious breaker of the law who is profiting from his acts.

Most game wardens are hard put to apprehend the man who is selling protected game or fish. To catch such a fellow, you have to be smarter than he is, which usually is plenty smart. The type of violation most wardens hate is the fish dynamiter and the deer jacker. Besides being hard to catch, either type may be dangerous—and you are always working in the dark.

The deer jacker cruises the roads in his car, switching his spotlight along the cover. When he sees a deer, he kills it and goes on about his business. He may slip back and dress out the deer in daylight, coming to his kill from the woods and not using the road. He can drag his deer back into the timber and hang it, and if the weather is cold he can take his time in getting it out.

Most jackers shoot and then drive on, coming back in an hour or so to see if the road is clear, in which case they get their deer and go on home. If the warden can pick them up with the deer, he has a case—provided the season is closed at the time. That is his best chance, but he must know who the guilty person is, for he can't stop and search every car that comes along the road.

Some one had been jacking deer. The warden got reports from farmers of hearing shots late at night from up on the mountain. No one had any idea who might be guilty in the small community. The killing had been going on all summer. The warden had walked miles along both sides of the road, and he had found where several deer had been killed—blood spots, patches of hair and the grass bedded down where the animal had been dragged to the road. According to hearsay, a deer was killed every three weeks by this man who liked "summer mutton." The law had one thing to go on—the shots were always heard about midnight.

It was a tough one, but this warden liked tough ones. Finally he hit upon a scheme that he thought would work. Two of the kills he had found were made in a small meadow in a saddle back on top of the mountain. Sparse hardwood second-growth edged the meadow before the heavy pine started. Deer browse was plentiful, and the meadow offered the best in grass.

BEER BOTTLE CAPS

When another kill was about due, the warden drove up on the mountain, coming in from opposite the near-by village. In his car he had an old mounted deer head. The glass eyes had been removed and in their place he had nailed beer-bottle caps that were good and bright. About a quarter of a mile from the meadow he drove his car back into an old woods road where it wouldn't be seen. Taking his rifle and a coil of rope, he shouldered his mounted deer head and headed for the meadow.

The warden cut off a small sapling and hung his deer head so that it was looking out through a clump of maple sprouts. He knew that his beer-bottle caps would catch the light from the spotlight, and he hoped his decoy would draw fire. From the deer head he ran a long rope off to one side, where he planned to await developments.

By 11:30 p. m. he was all set and ready. It was September and plenty cold. At two the next morning he took down his deer head and went home. The next night he had no better luck, but he stuck to the job and the third night he put up his deer head and hoped. The weather had turned colder and he had brought along a blanket and a lantern to keep warm. It's an old trick—a lantern between your feet, covered over with a blanket which goes up under your chin, will keep you warm in cold weather.

About 12:30 he saw a shaft of light playing along the mountain-side, first on one side of the road and then on the other. He knew his man was coming, and he hoped his deer head with its shiny eyes would do the trick. The car was crawling along slowly, but luck was with the warden, for it slid to a stop at the edge of the little meadow.

The light was moved slowly along the fringe of second-growth. The shaft passed over the warden, who was lying flat behind the cover. Then it paused, and almost instantly a gun roared. As the heavy load of buckshot cut through the brush, the warden jerked on his rope and the deer head went down. The spotlight went out and the car rolled on down the road.

The warden hadn't really been cold until then. He said he thought he would freeze waiting for the deer jacker to return. But success had made the fellow careless, and in less than an hour the car came crawling back and stopped. The light was switched out and the warden could hear talking. There were two of them! He eased out to the road as quickly as he could without making too much noise and worked up to the car. He didn't plan to let them find their deer, as that might spoil his case, although in this state it was against the law to shoot game from a highway, to shoot from a car and to carry a loaded gun in a car.

Switching the spotlight on the two men, he yelled, "Don't run, or I'll shoot! and walk back here."

They came back. The empty shotgun in the car was the only gun. They weren't vicious violators. One was the local justice of the peace and a deacon in the church; the other was the village doctor. The doctor took things as they came, but the deacon almost had hysterics—it was his car and his gun. In his frenzy he tossed aside friendship and insisted the doctor did the shooting.

The warden wasn't too hard. He let them go on home on their promise to appear at the County Court House the next day and plead guilty to a number of charges, including hunting without a license. The warden kept the gun, a few lodge cards and their drivers' licenses plus the spotlight from the car, just in case they might change their minds about pleading guilty. Whether they ever found out about the deer head I wouldn't know. Folks do say that deer jacking stopped in that section!

THE BLACKA HAND!

MY FRIEND the warden was just a little "hepped" on cats. Anyone who has a working knowledge of wild life and its enemies knows that the wild or half-wild house cat is a menace to all bird life, but Joe placed the cat at the top of the list and devoted much of his time to trying to exterminate all cat life. The law in his state read that anyone could, and it was the duty of all game protectors to, kill any cat found hunting birds. Joe took this law literally, and he worked at it overtime.

Cats are prolific, and any farm may easily acquire more felines than can be fed. The result is that the cats stray out into the fields and quickly find that young birds can be caught easier than mice—and maybe they taste better. Summer cottagers often go back to the city and leave a flock of cats to feed themselves. City dwellers, who should know better, will take a basket of kittens out into the country and leave them along the road, rather than kill "the cute little things." No animal is going to starve if it can help it, and the cats become experts at catching song birds and game birds. Most states have too many cats on the prowl through the countryside.

Joe aims to do his part in controlling this excess of cats. In his patrol car he carries a short-barreled 20-gauge shotgun sans stock. In other words, it is a long-barreled 20-gauge pistol. As he rides along the roads and sees a cat hunting birds he draws this weapon from the holster on the side of the car door, and there's one less cat to kill birds. Then he takes out a little book and enters the kill, for without this book some might doubt the extravagant figure he quotes when you ask him how many cats he has killed this calendar year.

Joe claims that unless you have made a study of the damage done by cats you can't conceive of the number of birds they kill. He has been studying them for years, his final investigation being over the barrels of his gun. He says that the day-hunting cats everyone sees when they drive through the country are as nothing compared to the cats working the coverts at night.

"Those two pinpoints of fire that your headlights pick up along the roads at night are cat's eyes, nine times out of ten," said Joe. "I can tell a cat every time by his eyes. You could, too, if you had studied them as I have. I used to cruise along, and when I'd see one I'd just slip my popgun out, and *wham*! I don't do that any more. I had the durnedest experience a man ever had. Ever since then I switch my spotlight over on the cat before I shoot.

"I'd been 'way up in the north end of my district one

night, trying to ride out a deer jacker. This bird would cruise the back roads with his spotlight on the cover, and when he'd shine a deer's eyes he'd crack down on it and then go on from there. If nothing happened, he'd sneak back in an hour or so to get his meat.

"That was the night I had the shock of my life. I was half asleep and as tired as a dog. You know where that big hill winds down past Turner Pond north of town? Well, I was gliding down that hill when I saw a cat on a stone wall on the left side of the road. As I had done thousands of times before, I reached over and got my gun, and *wham!*

"But that wasn't all! I heard glass break! I don't mean just a little glass, like a bottle; I mean all the glass in the world. I didn't stop. I never was so scared in my whole life! As I went on toward home I got to thinking, and I remembered that just back of that wall there was a little stone house. The sweat poured off me—cold sweat. I don't know how I could have done such a thing, but I had fired that load of chilled fours right at that house. I knew I had killed somebody!

"That house was just as much a part of the landscape to

27

me as Turner's Pond on the other side of the road. How I could have shot at it was more than I could figure out. I walked the floor all night long. Every once in a while my wife would wake up and ask me why I didn't come to bed, and then she'd go on snoring. Man, I was scared! I didn't know the fellow who lived there. All I knew was that he was an Italian stone-cutter who worked in the quarry at the bottom of the hill.

"Well, sir, if you want to suffer, just get it into your head that you've killed some innocent person, and come daylight you have to go down and own up that you did the dirty job. I was fit to be tied, and I expected to be tied tight.

"As soon as it began to get daylight I put on a brand-new uniform, shined up my badge a little and started out there. First, I drove straight by. Sure enough, there was the window, all stuffed full of rags and newspapers, but the coroner's car wasn't sitting out in front. I turned around at the top of the hill and came back down. It took a good deal of nerve, but I had to go in. I look big and tough, but don't you think I wasn't shaking like I had the palsy! You remember I plugged that fellow up on the new

Cemetery Road—when he tried to get me. That didn't bother me. This was different. At least, I hadn't killed everybody in the house, because someone had stuffed up the window.

"I load my own shells for that cat gun. I use fours chilled and a good jolt of powder. It's a wicked thing, and at that distance it would kill a horse. Several times on my way up those steps I came pretty near turning around and running. But I made it to the door and knocked.

"No one came. I knocked louder and said, 'Hello, in there!' Finally I heard someone moving around and a voice said: 'Mister policeman, please go 'way. Dat's alla right. We wanta no troub'. We goa 'way.'

" 'Open up,' I said, 'I want to talk to you.'

"I had to argue with him, but I finally got him to open the door, and I walked in. I wish you could have seen that room! It was right after prohibition had been passed and saloons were closed. This Italian had bought a huge crystal chandelier from some swank barroom. It had long and short pendants hanging singly and in clusters. My load of chilled fours had crawled through that glassware, and shattered glass was everywhere. All this time the Italian was jabbering, but I wasn't paying any attention to him. I was looking for the corpse.

"Over on the side of the room opposite the window was a bed, but all the covers had been pulled off and the whole room was torn up. It was evident these people were getting ready to move out.

" 'What's the matter here?' I asked, for want of something better to say.

" 'Tha's alla right,' jabbered the man. 'We goa 'way. Now, you goa 'way. We don'a want da police. Dey killa me, dey killa my wife if dey thinka we calla da police. Lasta night dey shoot at me an' my wife. Pleasa goa 'way. It's de Blacka Hand. Dey finda me out. Please you go.'

" 'Did they hit you?' I asked.

" 'Dey noa hita me. Dey shoota through da window. My wife, she and I we sleep in da bed. Da glass she fall everywhere all over me an' my wife. You pleasa go 'way.'

" 'How about your wife?' I asked. 'Was she hurt?'

" 'Naw, she nota hurt. I'm nota hurt. We goa 'way. Please you goa 'way.'

"I want to tell you that by this time I was feeling pretty good. There was a heavy load off my mind, and I didn't

30

object in the least to stooging for the Black Hand. I felt like buying this bird a new saloon fixture and redecorating his whole house for him, but I know that in the shape he was in there was no use talking to him. He was sure the Black Hand was after him, and that was that.

" 'Well,' I said, 'I guess I'll go and leave you, if that's what you want. You're sure, are you, that no one was hurt?'

" 'Sure,' answered Tony, 'tha's right. Nobody hurt.' Then he stopped short and a look of real grief came over his face. Shrugging his shoulders high and spreading his hands, palms forward, in a gesture of utter abandon, he sobbed: 'My poor kittay! She sleep at night on da window-sill. She get kill dead! Damna da Blacka Hand!' "

OPENING DAY

In the dim and distant past when ducks were plentiful and Federal regulations scarce, the waterfowl season used to open on September first. In those days the duties of the federal game wardens were chiefly to prevent spring shooting and the sale of game. In the spring months they were very busy, working long hours and traveling at night from one section of trouble to another. In most states the state game authorities cooperated, so that in the fall of the year the Federal wardens returned the favor by helping out the state men whenever possible.

One fall I waited daylight on the lower end of Sugar Lake, which lies in the bottomlands of the Missouri River east of Atchison, Kansas. The state warden from Missouri, located at St. Joseph, was a friend of mine and had been of much help to deputies I had working in his section. On this opening day he had asked for help in checking up the duck shooters who were sure to throng to this particular lake to collect the dividend promised by unsophisticated ducks.

Opening day anywhere is likely to be a slaughter. Young birds that have never been molested by man are easy pickings. It so happened that I was the only person available to help out on this job. The Federal law prohibited shooting until thirty minutes before sunrise, and it was also a violation to kill a wood duck. It is pitch dark thirty minutes before sunup, so that there was little to worry about on that score. But there were quite a few wood ducks in this section, which left the possibility of a federal case. The super-experienced wildfowler can identify a wood duck in the air almost as far as he can see it by its long square tail and rolling flight. However, there's not one duck hunter in fifty who can name these birds in flight.

Naturally I was hoping that no one would honestly make the mistake of killing a summer duck. That morning just before sunrise I saw one wood duck run the

33

gauntlet over the army of hunters, and I counted seventeen shots fired at him. He dodged not, neither did he flare. Instead of that he rolled on down the lake, high but in killing distance of any one skilled in overhead shooting. He passed directly over me where I stood at the end of the lake, and continued on to some haven along the Missouri River. Guns were popping everywhere, blue-winged teal were wheeling and darting all over the place. After thirty minutes of daylight, the battle was over. Some ducks had been killed; most of them had hied their way out of there. I walked back to the road and drove up to the head of the lake, where I was to meet the Missouri warden. He was on hand.

"If you'll just take a boat," he said, "and go down the north shore of this lake and check these birds for hunting licenses, I sure will be much obliged to you. I'll take the south shore, and we ought to be finished up by noon."

Sugar Lake grows hundreds of acres of great yellow waterlilies called yonkapins. I am told they are a true lotus. The big round leaves are often eighteen inches across. Instead of lying on the surface of the water, these lilies often extend a foot or two above it. Most of the duck hunters who knew their way around shoved their boats in this growth of lilies at the edge of open water and waited for the birds to pass by.

I started down the long strip of water, checking the boys for hunting licenses as I went. Most of them had conformed to the law and secured their licenses before coming out. Ahead of me I saw one boat being shoved rapidly through the lilies to the shore, and I knew that the two men in it didn't have licenses and the start they had on me would have made pursuing them futile.

Shortly afterward I saw where a boat had been shoved into the lilies, but apparently this fellow had gone so far back in, that he wouldn't have been able to reach any of the birds flying over open water with his shot. I stood up in my skiff and looked back among the lily-pads. There I witnessed one of the queerest sights I had ever seen.

The man was sitting in his skiff with a gun across his lap. He had on a blue serge suit, a white shirt and white collar, and a blue bow tie. I give you my word I am not exaggerating in the slightest—he wore a derby hat! I poled my skiff back in to him and asked if he had a license.

"License?" he questioned. "Why should I have a license? I am not a dog, and I have no dog."

Then I explained to him in detail that if he hunted game in the state of Missouri he was required by statute first to purchase a hunting license.

"Never heard of such a damn-fool thing," he replied. He was cocky.

Then it was my duty to tell him that under the circumstances I must place him under arrest.

"You can't do that!" he said.

"I have done it," I answered.

"Who are you, and what do you mean by coming in here and bothering me?"

I told him that I was a United States Federal Inspector under the Migratory Bird Law and that I was also a deputy Missouri state warden. I showed him a badge or two and let him read the inscriptions thereon. Then his demeanor changed.

"There must be some way we can settle this here," he said.

I told him there wasn't a chance and that I wanted him to stay right where he was until I went another half mile down the lake, when I would return and take him back to the landing. To make sure I didn't lose him, I took his gun and oars along with me.

When I came back, I had two other guns in my boat, and another boat was following me with a couple of the boys who had thought they could save a few dollars by not buying licenses. I told my friend with the bow tie to follow me, and never yet have I seen anyone have more trouble with a boat. I helped him get it out of the lily-pads, and when he took the oars in open water he was able to zigzag along behind me.

We reached the big Armour ice-house where most of the boats were kept, but the Missouri warden hadn't returned. My prisoner asked me to step to one side, saying that he would like to talk to me personally. He said: "I have never hunted duck before. I didn't want to hunt duck today, but I'm visiting a friend near here, and he insisted that I go. He put me into the lilies before daylight and left me, and I have no idea where he is. The mosquitoes nearly ate me alive, and I pushed the boat farther back into the rushes, thinking that maybe I could get away from them. I am a prominent attorney, and it won't do for me to be arrested for a violation of any kind. My position will not permit it. There must be some way this can be settled. I don't care what it costs—I am well able to pay."

I told him I was very sorry for him and that I hoped the statement he had just made wasn't intended to be a bribe, which would be a far more serious matter than shooting without a license.

About this time the Missouri warden appeared. "Well," he said, "I see you have some customers. Think I'd better shackle 'em and take 'em in to St. Joe, or do you suppose they'll plead guilty before the local justice here and make it easy for me?"

I looked at my friend in the derby hat, and he was shaking like a leaf. I have never seen a man in much worse physical shape. It wasn't cold, but I said to him: "Stand over there in the sun against the ice-house, out of the wind, where you'll be warm."

He did as I told him, but the sunshine seemed to have little effect on him.

The Missouri warden took out his book. "What's your name?" he asked.

The name was given.

"Where do you live?" asked the warden, and he noted that down in his book.

"What is your business?"

"I am general attorney for . . . " and he named one of the foremost railroads in the West, which at that time was having financial trouble.

"My God!" said the warden. "No wonder the road is in the hands of a receiver!"

A GOODA SPORT

Tony Napoleana is a plumber in my town. It so happens that I possess one of those kitchen sinks that get clogged up with distracting regularity. That's how

A GOODA SPORT

I happened to make the acquaintance of Tony. He was under my sink when I came in the back door, but he didn't stay there.

As soon as he saw me he began to grin and crawl out from under. Wiping his right hand on his overalls, he extended it to me. That hand didn't look exactly proper for presentation, but I took it and submitted to a hand-shake filled with the enthusiasm that makes these fellows so colorful. I couldn't understand what there was about me to call forth this greeting from a plumber who had been hired to blow out a drainpipe. I was also conscious of the high wage which these fellows get, and saw no excuse for him to stop work and shake hands with me on my time. As soon as Tony started to talk I discovered what the trouble was.

"I'm Tony. I'm a gooda sport! I know Dominick Di Pippo, who cuta da hair. He tella me 'bout you. He say you was one time a game-a-ward, but you gooda sport. I want you tella me 'bout da law. I shoota bird, a game-a bird on da ground, say laka pheasant—that breaka da law? I know that's not a gooda sport, but does that breaka da law?"

I told him that shooting a running pheasant was not

against the law, but that it wasn't a very sportsmanlike thing to do. Then I started to leave. But Tony was just getting started.

"I'm a gooda sport! No shoota chippy sparrow. I hunta quail, big-eyed snipe and dem odder bird you calla po-tridge—br-r-r-r-r-r!"

So exploded Tony, after which he paused for just the fraction of a second to get his wind and a fresh start. I couldn't stop him. I couldn't even get away from him. Time and again I started for the door, but he would stop me to launch into some fresh tale of his prowess with the scatter-gun. The poor sink suffered. I suffered both mentally and financially, but Tony raved on unchecked.

"I'm gooda sport! I got a setter-pointer, smooth laka hound. He finda quail—standa still, all stiff. He laka hunt big-eyed snipe you calla wooda roosta. Big-eyed snipe harda to hit. Tony bang—keela him, feel good all over.

"Thata setter-pointer of mine, sometime he geta big-eyed wooda roosta right by da nose. Wooda roosta mak a whistle w'en he fly. Data dog of mine jump and try to catcha big-eyed roosta. Mak me so dog-gone mad I beata hell out of him. I mak him standa still when a bird fly.

A GOODA SPORT

"You hunta pheasant? Bah! He's no game-a bird—he's a chick. Dominick Di Pippo he wanta me take my setter-pointer hunta pheasant. Dominick he laka hunta pheasant. Tony Ferrarro wot has dat rabbit hound Lucy, he tella me my dog no gooda hunta pheasant. Mak me so dog-gone mad! I think maybe Dominick thinka laka Tony Ferrarro. I get a big mad on, and tell Dominick I go witha heem where he says lotsa roosta pheasant. We go. Alla time Dominick keepa tella me I must no shoota hain pheasant and must no shoota roosta pheasant on da ground. He say gooda sport no shoota bird on da ground.

"He no have tella me dat. I'm a gooda sport. I no breaka da law. Game-a-ward say no shoota hain—I no shoot him. No gooda sport shoota a bird on da ground. I laka bird fly fast and dodge. Dominick, he keepa tell me no shoota hain, no shoota roosta on a ground. Maka me mad.

"We come to a swamp where Dominick say lotsa roosta pheasant. My setter-pointer he go out in swamp and runa round. By-a-by, he get alla stiff up, and I know he gota one. We go to him and geta all wet, and he gota nothin'. He go long some thirty-twenty feet maybe and say again he gota bird.

43

"He lie. He no hava roosta pheasant. Thata bird run through bog laka race-horse. Dat dog of mine he point da bird, and da bird she gone. He sniff and snuff around and go on and say he gota him again. He always lie. Dominick, he say maka him hurry. Dominick's a fool. I no maka my dog hurry. Take me two year maka him not hurry. We follow dat dog alla morning. I geta so dog-gone mad! Geta all wet in da swamp. My dog, he geta so tired and excite he shiva laka he vera cold, but he keep follow dat roosta pheasant.

"By-a-by Dominick say he run around 'way ahead and when roosta pheasant come outa swamp he kill her. I wait while he run downa other side of bogs. Justa then I see my setter-pointer; he start to trail to edge of bog and I go too. Then I see roosta pheasant; he come walka out of bog laka he own it. He no hurry. My setter-pointer he stopa dead. Tony no stop. I run as fast as I can. All da time I holla 'shoo, shoo, shoo!' I mak him run, but he no fly. I looka-back. Dominick he stand laka fool and look at me. Den he yell, 'Mak him fly! Don'ta you shoota heem on da ground.'

"Justa then thata roosta pheasant, alla bright red, yellow, green, brown, he jump ona rock wall and maka gobble at me. He go 'clucka-clucka-clucka.' Make any sport mad. I shoota one barrel a my gun in da air to maka heem fly. He hopa down on other side wall. I run to wall, and my setter-pointer he passa me and jumpa da wall. Then wot you think? Data bird fly? Naw! My gooda dog chase him out in pasture. He run justa laka rab'. He run ziga zag, and I thinka he's a crip. I shoulda shoota heem on da ground. That's alla right shoot a crip' bird on da ground. But I can no shoot less I shoota my dog. I say, 'Alla right, my gooda dog he catcha crip' pheasant.' Den wot you think? Data bird, he geta up and fly over trees too far to shoot.'

By this time Tony was almost exhausted. He was panting and mopping his face with a handkerchief which was none too clean.

"I say myself, soma day I come out here when Dominick stay home. I see roosta pheasant standa by stone wall. I gooda sport. I make heem fly. Laka hell!"

MOM'S DUCKS

In GAME-WARDEN work I never cease to marvel at the way men will lie when caught afoul of the law. This doesn't seem to apply to the hardened game-law violator. He may lie, but his stories will hang together and

it may take some doing to unravel them. The humorous liar is the man who has never been arrested before. He will tell one outlandish lie right after another, floundering around in an attempt to hit on something to convince the warden that he is innocent or the victim of circumstances.

One beautiful spring day I was driving through the sandhills of Nebraska with a local deputy. I wanted to see the country and the great quantity of birds that were gathered there.

We drove from one sandhill lake to another. Apparently there was no violation, as the birds were rafted in great numbers on all the available water.

While we were watching a great flock of canvasbacks diving and feeding we heard two shots over to the northwest. We got into the car and hied ourselves in that direction. There were no roads, and we drove right across the prairie. Leaving the car under the brow of a hill, we crawled up to the top and peeked over.

Below us lay a little pond of not over ten acres. On the near side was a duck blind. A pair of binoculars were put to work, and we saw that the blind was occupied by one man only and that he had half a dozen canvas decoys out in front of him.

"Let's go get him," said the deputy, but I suggested that we hang around awhile until we were sure that we had a case.

Any right-minded warden would rather keep a man out of trouble than get him in. I had coached everybody working for me along these lines. The purpose of a game warden is to protect game. If you can keep a man from killing it, you have done a better job than if you arrested that man after the game has been killed. Circumstances may alter cases, and I felt we should wait a while until we had something to go on that would impress the judge. Any man who had built a blind and put out decoys in the spring of the year, when all the newspapers had been filled with warnings, was certainly a wilful violator and should be dealt with accordingly.

So we lay on our bellies in the prairie grass and watched. Business was going to be good. A flock of spoonbills swept into the decoys, and our customer blazed away at them, killing one. He waded right out into the shallow water and got his bird, and then went about fifty yards below his blind where the bank of the pond was high. And there he stooped down and spent some time fiddling around. We couldn't see what he was doing. When he went back to the blind, he didn't take the duck with him.

"That's good enough," I said to the warden. "Let's go back to the car and drive down and get him."

Our prospective customer was so intent on passing fowl that he didn't hear us until we got right up to him.

"Having any luck?" the warden asked when we came up.

"I've taken a few pictures," the man replied. "It's against the law to shoot ducks at this time of the year."

"Oh, it is?" said the warden. "Then why have you got the gun?"

"Oh, I brought it along so as to kill a few crows or hawks. I wouldn't shoot a duck; I like to take pictures of 'em. Some day I hope to be able to take pictures of flying ducks like you see in the sporting magazines."

"Where's your camera?" asked the warden.

At this, he produced a No. 2 Brownie, which is a wonderful little machine for photographing baby at play in his pen or Towser as he sits up and begs for food, but which is wholly and totally inadequate for photographing an object moving at the speed of a flying duck.

"So you wouldn't shoot any ducks?" said the warden.

"No, sir, not me! I used to be president of the local sportsmen's association, and I'm just out here taking pictures of 'em."

"What were you doing down there by the bank a few minutes ago? As we came over the hill you were down there on your knees."

At this the fellow looked first at the warden and then at me. "Oh, that!" he said. "I saw a couple of boys poking around down there, and I just went down to see what they had been doing."

"What did you do with that duck you took down there with you?" asked the warden.

"Who, me? I didn't take any duck. I haven't had any ducks. I wouldn't shoot a duck."

The warden took the fellow's gun just as a matter of precaution, and we walked on down the shore. There, under the bank, was a muskrat hole, and out of that hole extended seven strings. As they were pulled out, one at a time, seven very muddy disreputable-looking ducks came forth. When this man killed a duck, he tied a string to its neck and, taking a stick, rammed it back into the muskrat hole, which lay half full of water.

"Well, bud," said the warden, "it looks to me like you got to go see the judge."

"I didn't kill those ducks," the man insisted. "I know nothing about it. I saw those boys fooling around down there, and I didn't know what they were doing."

"Don't lie any more," said the warden. "I'm gettin' dizzy. We saw you kill this drake spoonbill, and we watched you poke him back into that hole, and you're plumb out o' luck."

The fellow swallowed a couple of times and then he said: "Listen, fellows, I may have said some things that weren't true but, honest, listen, fellows, my mother's sick, and she asked me if I wouldn't get her some ducks. She just loves duck, and that's the only reason I'd shoot one."

The warden gathered up the ducks and, winking at me, said: "Come on, let's go. I'm afraid both you and Mom are out of luck, for she isn't going to get these ducks. We're going to give them to the judge and see if we can't bribe him to put you in jail."

DON'TA COME BACK!

WHEN Uncle Sam first took it upon himself to look after migratory birds, he operated under a broad measure aimed to guide and support the many state game departments. Seasons and bag limits were liberal. The states were supposed to make any further restrictions necessary to safeguard breeding stocks. Under the Federal law, any state could add further restrictions, but no state could extend shooting privileges beyond the broad limit of the Federal act.

Those charged with the enforcement of the Federal law were told to cooperate in every way with state enforcement officers and not to clutter up Federal courts with minor law infractions when violators could be tried and convicted under state laws. Federal game wardens were few in number, with District Inspectors here and there throughout the country to coordinate the work. The main burden of enforcing the Federal law was intended to fall on the broad shoulders of state game departments.

The second spring the law was in effect, I was working as a Federal District Inspector near Omaha, Nebraska. I was anxious to see a deputy warden who was working along the Missouri River. When I met my man, he told me that he had picked up an Italian who had broken both state and federal laws, and that he wouldn't be free to talk with me until he took this man before a justice of the peace and convicted him under the state law.

"What have you got him for?" I asked.

"Plenty," replied the officer. "He had two robins, four white-throated sparrows, a woodpecker, a meadow lark and a Plymouth Rock hen."

"Will he plead guilty?" I asked.

The warden didn't know. "All he will say is 'No speaka Engalais.' Furthermore," continued the warden, "he has 'phoned someone and talked to him in Italian and the trial has been set for eight o'clock this evening. You had better go along, as there may be some fun."

Guiseppi, the Italian, had been left at a police station for safe keeping, and we had just time enough to get a bite to eat and get back there for the trial. Several of this man's countrymen were there. The police judge was ready, and also there was present a dapper Italian attorney to see that the prisoner got a fair deal.

The attorney was smart. He talked good English—unless he got too excited. Then he might add an "a" here and there to a word, or drop a last syllable. The trial opened, and this lawyer painted a very vivid picture of his poor, misunderstood client. He told the court that the poor man was not long in our wonderful country, where men are free. Then, with flowery language, he paid tribute to the United States of America. He said his client could not talk or understand English, but as soon as he could he planned to take out his first papers and become a citizen of this grand, free country.

All this time the prisoner sat mute, with a blank expression on his face that showed plainly that he could not understand a word of what his friend was saying. The attorney, with much arm waving and shoulder shrugging, explained in detail that in Guiseppi's home in Italy there were no such laws that forbade a man to take wild birds for food. All his life Guiseppi had hunted, and it was only natural that when he came to America, the land of the free, he would wish to continue this sport that furnished him with food for his wife and babies. Had this son of Italy only known that it was against the law to shoot birds, he would never have done so.

By the time the lawyer was half through with his recital, he had me feeling sorry for the prisoner. I might have been in favor of turning him loose if the warden hadn't whispered to me, "How about the domestic chicken he shot in somebody's barn-yard. Do they do that in Italy?"

I looked at the judge. He didn't seem to be particularly impressed with what he was hearing. In fact, I wasn't sure he was hearing all of it. He looked tired and sleepy to me, like a fellow who was bored and wished the whole thing was over with.

Putting on a grand flourish, the attorney concluded his speech with a request for clemency. Then he entered a plea of guilty and threw his client on the mercy of the court.

Without changing expression the judge boomed out, "One hundred dollars or thirty days in jail!"

Guiseppi jumped from his chair, waving his arms around and shouting, "Thees a hella free countree!"

The judge boomed out once more, "Fifty dollars for contempt of court!"

With that the Italian attorney rushed toward his client, knocking over a chair and shouting, "Don't come back, Guiseppi. Don'ta come back! Pleasa don'ta come back!"

The fellow stood with a scowl on his face, mumbling

and muttering to himself. From his pocket he brought a roll of bills that looked very substantial. Slowly he stripped off one hundred and fifty dollars, laying the money on the clerk's table before the bench. Then he looked up at the judge with a sneer and said, "Every day I taka my leetle gun and shoota chippy bird."

"Thirty days in jail for contempt of court!" roared the judge. "See if you can shoot that with your little gun. Take him away! Next case."

HUNT DEAD!

ONE spring, shortly after it had been made illegal to shoot migratory waterfowl anywhere in the United States or Canada, a Federal game warden was patrolling the Arkansas River. A road paralleled the river some half a mile distant. This game warden, being of a lazy and retiring temperament, was satisfied to drive along this road in his curtained Ford and trust to his knowledge of waterfowl to tell whether anyone was hunting on the river.

Big flights of ducks were traveling both up and down the stream, and any man could tell by watching them whether or not they were being shot at. It would have been impossible to hear shooting on the river above the noise from the motor. Apparently no one was cheating, as the birds flew steadily. Then a bunch was seen to flare, not badly, but as though they had seen something that might possibly harm them.

"Those birds weren't shot at," commented the warden to himself, "but I think I'll stick here a few minutes and watch the next flock or two."

Several high bunches passed along the river without wavering; then a small flock set their wings as if to alight. Down behind the trees they coasted out of sight from the warden's car; then they came up, climbing to safety. The warden switched off the motor in time to hear the rattling volley of shots from the river. One bird scaled down in the wheat field between the road and the river. This bird, a drake mallard, was picked up by the warden and cached along a fence to be used later as evidence if needed.

Coming to the edge of the woods facing the river, the officer gingerly looked up and down, trying to locate his quarry before the law breakers saw him. This is a very good plan, as many boastful violators of the game laws are apt actually to bounce out of a blind and run if approached by a stranger when they are bravely shooting ducks that law-abiding gunners fear to molest.

All the officer could see were a half dozen or more live decoy ducks tied in shallow water near the end of a flat bar about thirty yards off shore. This was all he wanted to see, for he knew that the gunner, or gunners, were well hidden close by.

For many yards back the river bank was covered with a heavy growth of slough grass, which had been pressed down by the ice when the river broke up in the early spring. No cover high enough to conceal a man was visible, and no blind was in evidence as the officer approached the shore of the river. When within fifty yards of the river bank, he saw a beautiful black and white setter rise out of the grass and stand wagging her tail in greeting. Her notice of the officer caused three men to rise from a pit they had dug in the sand.

"What luck?" asked the game warden.

"Haven't had a shot yet," lied one of the men.

"We just this minute got here," was the lie told by the second man, and the third fellow could not think of any lie just then, so he stood mute.

The officer looked over the ground carefully. No empty shells were in evidence, and no dead ducks were piled behind the blind. It was plain that these three fellows were the real sneaking kind and had been covering their tracks well, so as to fool an officer of the law should one show up. The empty shells had promptly been thrown into the river, and the game as killed had been well hidden.

"I am a Federal officer charged with enforcing the game laws," was the next remark made by the warden. "You men leave your guns where they are and step up here. I want to talk to you."

The three gunners complied; then the warden, by way of precaution, jumped down in the blind and unloaded all three guns. Should a fuss start, a loaded gun is apt to complicate matters.

"Where are your ducks?" was the warden's first question after license numbers had been taken and names and addresses carefully noted for future reference.

"We haven't killed a duck nor shot at one," lied all three men in unison.

Then the third fellow, who up to the present had had little to say, became suddenly possessed of extensive conversational powers, prompted, no doubt, by mental visions of Federal judges. "Honest, mister," he insisted, "we just came. We ain't shot; we didn't know it was against the law. We heard the law had been knocked out. We've got a friend who said the state legislature of Kansas had declared the Federal law unconstitutional. Another friend of ours knows the Attorney-General of Missouri, and he says the law isn't any good. If we'd known there even was such a law, we wouldn't have come out—would we, fellers?"

The "fellers" were profuse in their insistence that they would not have thought of coming out if they had known they were breaking the law by so doing.

HUNT DEAD!

This particular warden had been at the game for some time, and he was familiar with most of the tricks of the trade. As it is just as much a violation of the Federal law to hunt ducks during the closed season as it is to kill them, he already had a good case—men in a duck blind with loaded guns and decoys out in front of them, and one dead duck, which he could swear was shot and killed from the immediate vicinity of this blind.

The conclusion of the officer was that dead ducks were not very far away, and he knew full well they would strengthen his case. Therefore, he began to search around in the grass. His efforts registered a blank, and one of the gunners became just a little impudent in his comments.

When the warden first started to search the near-by landscape for dead ducks, considerable interest was shown by the setter, who was promptly ordered to lie down. Now, if there was one thing this warden could do, it was to get on good terms with a shooting dog. Pointers and setters alike seemed to sense his friendship, and this particular setter was no exception to the rule. The warden had been petting her and playing with her from the first and was soon considered by the dog as one of the gang.

HUNT DEAD!

It was not a new trick in his annals of game-law enforcement, and the officer felt sure it would work. Apparently he had given up his search for the birds, satisfied that the men were telling the truth, and was now simply standing around visiting and petting the dog. Without the slightest warning of his intention, he spoke to the dog in the commanding voice which well-broken bird dogs love to obey: "Hunt dead! Look 'em up! Dead bird, old girl!"

The dog bounded forward at the sweep of the warden's arm ordering her on, but before she had made her third jump she heard her master's voice yelling: "Come in here to me, you blank-blank-blanketty-blank! I'll break your neck if you move from me again."

It is very doubtful if this setter loved to obey her master's voice, but it was also very evident that she had learned it was best in the long run. So this dog, named "Happy," slunk back with anything but a happy air about her and dropped in the grass at her master's feet, only to receive a foot rolled across her neck for her obedience.

A game warden should never lose his temper, but this one did. "Take your foot off that dog, or I'll knock you loose from the earth," he shouted, and the foot came off.

"Now," he continued, "I'm going to tell you fellows something. I have case enough to load you all in my car and take you to the nearest police station, and ask to have you held for investigation. Then comes a trip to the nearest United States Commissioner and then high bond, which you will furnish or go to jail. You are guilty, just as guilty as you can be. You have ducks hidden all over this side of the river, under the grass, where I doubt if you could find them yourself without your dog.

"Now, I'll tell you what I'm going to do. I'm going to win myself back into Happy's confidence, if I can, and have her bring those ducks in to me. If one of you so much as opens his mouth to prevent the dog working for me, we are all going to start for the nearest jail. If you behave yourselves, I will simply file your case with the Department, and later you can arrange with the United States Attorney to plead guilty and avoid lots of unpleasantness which you are sure to experience if you use poor judgment.

"Come, Happy," said the warden.

As Happy came, casting doubtful glances back at her master, he said not a word. Considerable petting was indulged in, and then Happy and the warden walked down the river bank together in the direction in which Happy had started when her master called her back.

"Hunt dead!" said the warden, and Happy, with one reproachful glance at her master, started out into the grass. Once she stopped and looked back at him, but as he said nothing she went ahead, and from under a big tussock of grass she pulled a big, long-necked pintail drake.

The warden walked back to the three men, and when Happy delivered the bird he ordered her back for another. Each bird was taken from a different place. "Dead bird! Go get 'em," said the warden, and Happy kept proudly bringing them in until the pile had taken on sizable proportions.

"Dead bird! Bring 'em in," repeated the warden, but Happy came back the second time without a bird and stood wagging her tail while her eyes said plainly. "That's all, Boss. Hide 'em again."

Seventeen dead ducks—eleven pintails and six mallards. As the warden tied them up to carry them away for what the court calls *prima facie* evidence he turned to Happy's owner and left with him this farewell charge: "You've got a right to a good dog. She is in no way to blame for getting these ducks for me. You could not expect her to do otherwise. If I hear that you have mistreated her for her part in this affair after I leave, I intend to come back when business is dull and beat hell out of you! Good-day."

BAILEY'S BULL

I'M AFRAID of bulls. I don't care what kind of bull it is or how trustworthy its reputation—I don't like 'em. It isn't just a phobia; I have had experience with several of them and want no part of any bull. If you look down out of a tree at a mad bull once or twice, you'll get to dislike the brutes fervently.

This yarn of ducks and game wardens also has to do with bulls. In fact a bull plays the leading role, as a Federal warden tries to pick up a cagey spring shooter.

"We can come in from the river and get this bird red-handed," said the warden. "It would be a cinch if it were not for a bull, but we can handle him."

This deputy had been spending a considerable time trying to catch a violator who lived along a lake lying in the bottom lands of the Missouri River. The spring shooter operated at daylight, usually pouring five shots out of an automatic at fowl resting along the shore. That wasn't all. He was undoubtedly market shooting, as it was known that his wife frequently went to Kansas City with a couple of suitcases.

"It's as simple as two plus two," continued the warden. "This smooth guy who thinks he can't be caught lives right on the lake bank. He never hunts, and therefore he thinks he is above suspicion. Furthermore, he has friends who warn him by 'phone when I arrive at the other end of the lake. When I'm there he doesn't shoot.

"Now, here is the pay-off. This fellow's wife has been going to Kansas City about three times a week, something very unusual. Answer—bootlegging ducks. I haven't had a chance to do much on this end of the case, but I know it would be hard going. What we want to do is get this bird who is doing the shooting.

"My plan for the morning is this. We'll take a boat and cross the river and come into the lake from the west. Unless I miss my guess, I'll be holding a candle for him to aim by in the morning. There's just one possible hitch to my plan, but I'm usually lucky and I'm not worrying any."

"What's this hitch?" I asked.

"It's the bull. You see, I've been down there today looking the ground over so there will be no slip-up in the morning through any fault of mine. When we cross the river, we land near the outlet from the lake. The first quarter of a mile is heavy willow and cottonwood. Then we cross a road and must follow along the outlet through a pasture owned by a fellow named Bailey. This pasture runs clear up to the lake. Our man does his shooting about an eighth of a mile around a bend in the shoreline.

"Bailey has a herd of Jersey dairy cows, and with them runs about the meanest Jersey bull you ever saw. I've been told he's a mankiller and that even Bailey is afraid to go in this pasture without a pitchfork. Last shooting season this bull caught a couple of fellows going through the pasture and nearly gored one of them to death. Both finally escaped by swimming the outlet. Since that time Bailey has kept his land posted, but of course this won't bother us."

"Which won't bother us," I asked, "the posting or the bull?"

"Neither," replied the warden. "We can keep close to the outlet; and if worst comes to worst, we can take to the water and swim to safety. If we could only wade this stream, we could go down the other side; but I walked the full length of it, and there isn't a chance in the world of crossing that pass without getting over our boots. These mornings are too cold to get wet unless we have to do so to disappoint Bill Bailey's bull."

The next morning was a cold one. The thermometer must have been well below $32°$, for the mud along the river bank was almost stiff enough to hold us up. As our boat landed at the mouth of the outlet a big full moon was just sinking behind the bluffs to the west. A blanket of inky blackness was settling rapidly, but the warden knew the lay of the land, and we quickly fought our way through the heavy willow growth to the road where the cow pasture began. It was good to be out of the boat. The exercise of our walk had stopped our teeth from chattering, and instead I could feel the perspiration starting under my hat band.

Once in the pasture, the going was easier, and my friend quickened the pace he was setting. "Take your time," I cautioned him. "There's no use in working up a sweat that will freeze us to death while we're waiting for your man to start shooting."

"It'll be time enough to slow up after we are out of this pasture," the deputy whispered back to me as he kept on along the edge of the water.

The rate at which we were going didn't appeal to me. I knew that, if it had to be done, we could either cross the narrow stream of water along which we were walking or we could kill the brute. My forty-five would stop any bull. Of course, the gun wouldn't be used unless it meant saving one of us from getting seriously hurt, as I had no desire to purchase an expensive Jersey bull for target practice. "Let him race on," I thought to myself as I slowed down to a more moderate gait.

It was about as dark a night as I ever saw. Immediately I slowed up, the warden's form disappeared. Then I heard a cow bell off to my left. It was only tinkling at first, but as I listened it took on a steady clanging and I thought I could hear hoof beats. Now I knew I could, and I started on the run to catch up with the warden. In the darkness I almost ran over him.

"My God, we're in for it!" he whispered as he grabbed my arm.

We could hear the thud of hoofs on the frozen ground. There were several cows coming along with the bull. Nearer and nearer came the clanging bell. Now, farmers don't put bells on a bull. Some reliable old cow was wearing that bell, some cow that could be depended on to lead the herd. Undoubtedly she was behind the bull, following along with some more of the herd to see the fun. The sound of the bell could not be counted on to tell us how

73

far away the bull was from goring us at the present moment. Some one had told me once that a bull always closes his eyes just before he hits you and that it is a simple matter to sidestep him.

Our situation was a different one. How could you sidestep something you couldn't see, even if that something did have its eyes closed and couldn't see you? Maybe that bull was closing his eyes right now. We had no time to lose, for the hollow thuds of many hoofs were now painfully close to us.

"Quick!" I called. "We must take the water."

Just as I said this I heard a splash, then a gasp, and more splashing, and from out of the dark I heard the warden's voice.

"Damned fine trick to do! Hurry, but be careful and don't fall down, for I don't believe it's over your head here. Jumping jimminy cripes, but this water is cold."

The first three steps I took broke a thin coating of ice with water only up to my knees. Then I went in up to my waist. I'll never forget that sensation as the ice-water ran down into my hip boots and seemed to cut me half in two. The next step, and the water was well over my stomach.

My breath was being pushed out of me. I could not have spoken if my life had depended upon it. Gasp after gasp escaped my lips as the water got deeper and deeper. Of one thing I was certain—I heard a wrangling, clanging cowbell and the roar of hoofs on frozen soil.

I was holding my forty-five and a box of matches high over my head. An outdoor man does such a thing instinctively, for I had no knowledge of the act until I was climbing out on the opposite shore. At the deepest place the water just lapped my chin. As I reached firm ground the cavalcade of hoofs stopped where we had been but a second or two ago. The bell stopped except for a tinkle or two as the old milk cow fed along the opposite shore.

"Pretty close call, I'll say," chattered the warden as he pulled handsful of dry grass with which to start a fire.

Plenty of dry driftwood lay piled high and dry along the bank, and it was only a short time until we had a good fire going. We stripped to the skin, wrung our clothes dry, and put our outer garments on again to protect us from the wind while we dried our socks and underwear over the fire. As we sat crouched before the blaze, turning socks and rearranging underwear on a framework of sticks we had constructed, I commented that I was glad my hat was dry.

"Mine's in the drink," dryly stated the warden. "I lost the thing when I took a header. I'll have to look for it when it gets light."

Just then five shots rang out from the lake. They poured out into the morning stillness just about as fast as a man could run them from a gun.

"Hell!" said the warden, "he's beat me again, but I'll get him yet."

A streak of grey was showing in the east. All but a few of the stars had faded. The air was filled with the whir of flying waterfowl. A great blue heron squawked as he passed overhead on his way to the river.

We had put on our underwear, which was dry, and were devoting our attention to drying our shirts and trousers. A small flock of green-winged teal dropped into the water near us and sat with heads upstretched looking at our fire. We kept very quiet, and they soon decided all was well and started feeding and preening their feathers.

"Hand me that other boot," whispered my friend, and with a splash and a whir our ducks were up and away.

76

It was now light enough so that we could follow them with our eyes for some distance before we lost them in the haze of early morning.

"Well, I'll be horn-swaggled and double dod-gasted," burst out the warden.

I looked in the direction in which he was gazing, and there, right across the outlet from us, stood an old gray mare with a bell fastened around her neck, while near her fed several other horses!

BLOWOUT TONY

Tony mended tires, and over his shop in letters two feet high he named himself "Blowout Tony." Whenever there was the slightest excuse he left his place of business in charge of others and went shooting. He carried a high-grade Parker double-barreled hammerless shotgun, and his bags of game, many times looked over by the warden, showed that he could use that gun.

Tony was my friend up to a point. I had never caught him breaking the law, but I often had my suspicions. A warden can't operate on suspicions. On unfortunate occasions I had found friends of Tony's in violation of the conservation code, and they had each and every one paid a fine. Tony would be in the party, but he was always within the law. Neither Tony nor his friends were song bird shooters in the strict sense that they went afield to kill small songsters. They were after game birds and rabbits, and if any of them shot a robin or a flicker it was just a passing fancy and done in a moment of inadvertence.

There was one thing that Tony held against me: I wasn't a regular game warden. Many years before I met Tony I had given up the game-warden business as a steady diet. But I kept deputy commissions here and there, and when I was hunting I checked up on the boys when I thought the occasion demanded it. The professional hunters of song birds always irked me, and I would quit hunting any time to land one of these fellows.

Tony felt that I was butting into business that didn't concern me when I checked up on him or his friends. He told me so, many times.

"Some-a day, by gees, you get ina troub'."

Tony was very profane, and it is almost impossible to tell any story about him without using his colorful expressions. Without profanity, Tony would have been practically mute.

One fall morning Harry Shedd and I were hunting woodcock in northern Westchester County in New York state. We were in an area filled with alders and blackberries, with bog swamps here and there and some patches of open pasture. The leaves were still on the alders, and in many places you couldn't see twenty feet in front of you. It was perfect woodcock cover, but we weren't flying any woodcock. We kept plugging away, for that year the woodcock season opened ahead of any other game and there was nothing else to hunt.

Just before noon I heard voices coming down through the alders ahead of us and to our left. I listened a moment to this talking back and forth and made up my mind that this hunting party was a crowd of Italian song-bird shooters. During the morning I had heard a few scattered shots —just single shots, no quick doubles. This sounded like song-bird shooters; so I headed toward them to see what I might see.

It was hot and sticky, and spider-webs were everywhere. Getting through the alders and swamps was real work. I hurried as fast as I could, as I wanted to come up with this crowd before the boys passed in front of me. From their voices I could tell they were going through the cover at right angles to the line which Shedd and I had been following. Just as I burst through a particularly heavy piece of cover I came face to face with Tony.

"Hel-lo!" said Tony. "What you kill?"

"Nothing," I replied. "What kind of luck have you fellows been having?"

Now, Tony's coat stuck out in the back, and my guess was a couple of illegal pheasants at least, for there were pheasants in the cover and the season on these birds was closed. Maybe he had some song birds, and maybe not. Anyway, it looked interesting, but before we could reach the point of finding out just what the coat contained I heard a fellow in the alders above and in front of us yell, "Wooda cock!"

Tony jumped on a near-by stone wall where he could see better and, as anyone would, I got ready to shoot if the bird came hurtling over the alders toward us. Then there was a shot from another member of the party and Tony said:

"That damna fool! By gees, he missa that wooda cock."

"Where did it go?" I asked.

"Get up here on disa wall," said Tony. "I show you right where he seta down."

Being a woodcock hunter first and then a game warden, I climbed up on the wall.

"See that little maple tree on de other side of dis swamp? Right dere he drop in. You go geta him. I standa right here and tell you where to go."

No woodcock hunter is going to pass up a chance like that; so I started in my most enthusiastic manner. I fought the bogs and the spider-webs, and in time I reached the little maple tree and walked around it. I was hunting with a scatter-brained puppy, and I called him and had him look. Neither of us could flush a bird from that cover. I looked back, and Tony was still on the wall.

"Righta there, where you are," he called. "Looka good."

Another hunter came out of the alders about this time on Tony's side of the swamp and stood looking at me. He was apparently the fellow who did the shooting.

"Where did that bird go that you shot at?" I asked. "I keela heem," he replied, and he held up the woodcock to show me.

"There must have been two of them," I thought, but as I couldn't raise the second bird there was nothing else to do but go back and see what Tony had in his coat.

Tony waited, and when I got there he was grinning.

"Too bad you could no make heem fly," he said, still grinning.

I commenced to see things as they really were. I looked at Tony's coat, and it was as flat as the back side of a barn. He saw me look at his coat and then he said: "You pretty smart game-a-ward, huh? You think you pretty smart. You not so doldam smart!"

I called up my dog and had him look dead. He was pretty good at this, but he never checked once as he covered the near-by area. I thought some of tearing down the stone wall. I thought of a lot of things. But I knew there was no use. If Tony had had pheasants or a pheasant in his coat, another member of the party was far away with the game by this time.

"So long, Tony," I said. "I'll be seein' you again some-time."

"Sure Mike," answered Tony. "You not so smart you think you are, and soma day you get in mucha troub'."

BOOTS

Cᴇʀᴛᴀɪɴ of our citizens always feel that they can buy their way through. The man charged with enforcing conservation laws meets up with these individuals frequently. The usual procedure is for the guilty one to explain in very confidential tones that, because of his social or financial standing in the community, he cannot afford to be arrested and therefore and whereas he is prepared to settle on the spot.

I remember hearing a game protector in Westchester County, New York, tell of an experience that was a little off the beaten track. It seems he had arrested the Italian consul, or at least someone high in the consular service. This man was shooting robins at the edge of a county park. A chauffeur in livery waited on the road in an expensive foreign car.

So busy was this gentleman, shooting song birds, that my friend walked right up to him and caught him red-handed. He was astounded to learn that he was doing anything wrong. He talked perfect English and explained in great detail, accompanied by appropriate arm-waving, that in his country it was legal to shoot all small birds. The warden, having heard all of this many times before, was probably a little hard-boiled. "Come on, get going," he said. "We've got to go to see the judge."

The song-bird shooter smiled rather confidently.

"I didn't know what was coming next," said the warden. "He seemed happy about something. Then he reached in his pocket and pulled out a roll of bills that would choke a cow. Holding this bank roll in his left hand, he started peeling them down. First came tens. Slowly he stripped off five, letting them hang from his hand, all the while grinning at me. Then came twenties—there were seven of these. Underneath the twenties were fifties. My eyes began to pop out until you could knock them off with a stick. After he had slowly stripped down four fifties, I yelled at him, 'Good God, man, stop! You're reaching my price!' He may have been a diplomat, but he was a sorry-looking one after the judge got through gettin' him told. At that he saved a lot of money, for his fine was chicken feed compared to what he wanted to give me."

Years ago I was offered a bribe that was a little out of the ordinary. The Federal Government had recently put the clamps on the spring shooting of waterfowl. Some of the boys didn't want to stop. We had had numerous reports of violations west of a little town on the Missouri side of the Big Muddy. In those days there was no finer place for wild waterfowl. Big Slough was undoubtedly the old river bed, but in the memories of the oldest inhabitant the Missouri River had always flowed far to the westward.

When the fall flight is on, these waters accommodate a score or more of gunners, and every one usually gets a few birds. It is so situated that every bunch of traveling ducks that come down the river is sure to pass over it. Once over it and they see what wonderful attractions Big Slough holds for them, they are sure to stop.

Migrating birds follow the river on their way south and again when they return to the north in the spring. The main north and south course of the river is directly in line with Big Slough, but about a mile north from the upper end of the slough the river bears off to the west, flows south again and comes back east about two miles south of the lower end. The river really makes a big detour around Big Slough, with the result that the ducks from their vantage point up in the air, take the straightaway. In the spring, when no shooting is legal, this water is just a living writhing mass of wild ducks. I know of no greater sight when the spring flight is on. Often I have seen large flocks of ducks coming in to alight on some favored part of the slough, and I have wondered if they could possibly find space on the water.

This old river bed was a "natural" for violators. The topography of the country was such that, unless a warden knew the lake section equally as well as the gunner, he had small chance of catching him. Small chutes and bayous ran off into the willows from the main water. Some of these could be waded with hip boots, and some could not be waded at all. While I doubt if there were six feet of water anywhere in Big Slough, the mud in some parts seemed bottomless. A violator of the game laws who knew the lay of the land certainly had a warden at a big disadvantage.

Investigations proved that the illegal shooting took place nearly every morning and through the night on moonlight nights. At least two men were at it, for one fellow always shot six shots from a pump, while the other fired two quick shots from a double gun. The shooting all took place at the lower end of the slough, where the willows were very thick. All a man had to do was to come to the edge of these willows, let drive into a flock of sitting birds, gather the dead, and step back out of sight. No game warden on earth could catch him unless luck played with the law or he learned the movements of his man and picked him up on the way out.

I had had several deputies working in this section without success. Apparently some one in the town tipped the fellows off and no shooting took place when a warden was on the job. I had hunted ducks on Big Slough in past years, and I knew the country pretty well; so I decided to take a crack at the fellow myself. Instead of going to the near-by town, I got off the train at the first station to the south. It was 2 a. m. by the station clock after I had had lunch and a cup of coffee. With my boots over my back I started up the railroad track.

It was not daylight until about five-thirty; so there was no occasion for me to hurry. Without any trouble I found the path through the willows alongside which the boys had roosted for several days and nights and which they were sure our duck hunter used in going out to the slough. The path had been traveled sufficiently so that it was not difficult to follow in the starlight.

When I reached the edge of the open water, I stepped

to one side and found a very comfortable seat on an old cottonwood log. A heavy green willow growth had sprung up around this log, so that I was fairly well hidden, especially from the rear. There was water all around the log, but it was only a few inches deep. The mud, however, was deep enough to necessitate extreme caution to keep from making such a racket that every duck would be scared off the slough.

A few birds rose as I came in, but I could hear hundreds more close to me on the open water. The meowing quack of the redhead vied with the guttural note of the scaup, or bluebill. As I sat there waiting for daylight, I distinguished, besides the mallard call which was common, the notes of the gadwall, green-winged teal and pintail and also the whistle of the widgeon.

As day started to break the birds began to move. A constant whistle of wings came from overhead, and flocks of birds headed on north could be heard rising from the water while new bunches came splashing in. What nature lover would not have enjoyed being with me on that log in the early morning light with wild birds, unconscious of my presence, almost alighting on top of me! It was now light enough that I could occasionally see long strings of ducks against the sky in the east.

A shoveller swam inside the willows and fed past me, not three feet from the log on which I sat. I could identify her by the small head and enormous spoon-shaped bill. She was clucking away with her spring love note that soon brought a drake to the open water near her. Whether she joined him or not I do not know, for just then I thought I heard a slight, unnatural noise behind me. Now I knew I did.

Some one was coming along the path and had reached the mud. Ever so slowly and carefully he was raising his feet out of the muck and gently placing them in again. He was doing a much better job than I had done thirty minutes previously, for not a duck flushed as he approached. Now he was even with me, and I could see his outline plainly. Carefully he worked past me and a little closer to the open water. There he stood as though frozen and not ten feet from me.

It was now light enough to distinguish the birds fairly well on the water before us. Once he raised his gun toward a solid mass of bluebills, but he did not shoot. I thought first I would stop him before he pulled the trigger and save that many birds; but then I thought of the time and money spent trying to land this fellow, and decided it was far better to let him shoot and get a case that would prove air-tight before the court.

A raft of redheads was working in toward us, and I could see that he was watching them. Again his gun came slowly up to his shoulder. He held it there for a second or two, and then—"*bang!*" one shot on the water and "*bang!*" the other barrel as the ducks raised. The shots sounded unusually loud, much more so than would have been the case during the shooting season with guns being fired on every side. The roar of the rising waterfowl was like thunder as the scared birds winged their way out of danger.

"Hand me that gun," I said quietly. "You are under arrest. Now sit down on this log by me and keep still."

He started to say something, but I told him to keep quiet. You see, I thought there might be another victim, and we might as well wait a while with the hope of doing the job right.

I counted nine dead redheads on the water slowly floating in toward us and three crippled birds swimming in the

93

opposite direction as fast as their condition would let them. The gun I was holding across my knees was a beautiful little 12-gauge Sauer hammerless, an arm that any one would be proud to own. My catch must be a wealthy fellow.

I turned to size him up and he started to talk, but I told him again to keep quiet and stay down by me on the log. Every time he started to talk I'd shut him off. Apparently he was a man of considerable means, a German who had not been in this country for very long. This I gathered from the few broken sentences he had been able to get out.

The weather was mild, but the fellow was shaking as though he had the ague. I had seen men affected that way before. I had taken his gun, he was under arrest, and his nerve had left him. His teeth were chattering and his face was chalky white. I saw him look at the handcuffs snapped on my belt, and an extra chill went through him. I actually felt sorry for him.

Almost immediately after the shooting the ducks began dropping back in the slough. The water was soon covered with them. What a sight, as the rising sun shot its first gleams of gold over the vari-colored mass! I had about given up catching another violator and decided we had better leave in order to catch the first train south, for I planned to go immediately to the nearest United States Commissioner and have the violator bound over to the United States Grand Jury.

The man was wearing about the finest pair of hip boots that I had ever seen. They were deep flesh color, had round tops and came clear to his crotch, though he was a tall man. The rubber looked especially good. You could see its great elasticity when he bent his knees. I reached over and felt the quality; he flinched and started to speak, but I stopped him. I looked over at my own boots, which had been patched and re-patched. By way of breaking my silence and letting my prisoner know that I was now ready to move, I remarked, "That's a mighty fine pair of boots you've got on."

"Gott knows, if dat's all you vant, mister, you can haff dem," he replied. And before I could stop him he had pulled one boot off and was handing it to me. That is the only bribe I ever had offered to me that I had a hard time turning down. I'm still sorry I didn't accept those boots, say as a gift from one duck hunter to another.

WANTED!

A GROUP of Federal game wardens was gathered one night in a hotel room in Wichita, Kansas, trying to out-lie each other. Most of the experiences related had to do with the unmatched shrewdness or the great courage of the narrator, but occasionally a story cropped out that had its humorous side.

"The darnedest experience I ever had in my whole life while enforcing game laws happened right here near this city," said one of the boys. "It cost me one hundred big round dollars, and I'll never forget that bird as long as I live—how he looked and how he acted. Believe me, I was plumb up against it!

"It was in the spring of the year, and I had been told to patrol the Arkansas River in the vicinity of Wichita, Kansas. We were short-handed, and my instructions were to get over the ground as quickly as I could, not to make any arrests of violators where my time would be taken up with court procedure, but simply to get the information—get the evidence and be able to lay my hands on the spring shooters during the slack season in the summer.

"I had hired a livery car and a boy driver at Wichita, and at the first streak of light we were rolling along a sand road which paralleled the river on the north. It was colder than blazes! There was snow on the ground with the thermometer around freezing, and a south wind was blowing that got right into your bones.

I was counting on using the time-worn trick of watching the birds to tell where the gunners were. As long as the flocks of wild ducks, mostly mallards and pintails, flying up and down the river held steadily to their course, I felt pretty confident that no one was operating beneath them.

"We had covered some fifteen miles when I noticed the birds flaring up. I stopped the car and sat there and watched perhaps half a dozen flocks. I heard no shooting, but every flock of birds towered into the air when they reached a certain point on the river.

"I had about concluded that the ducks were being frightened by some object that looked like a man, for many of them seemed low enough to draw the fire of any gunners who might be stationed in that vicinity, and still not a shot was fired. Just as I had about decided to drive on I heard four or five shots in rapid succession, apparently fired at birds too low for me to see on account of the timber that fringed the river bank. Evidently the shots were successful, as I saw no ducks come into view above the trees after the shooting was over.

"Telling my driver to wait for me, I struck off across the two hundred yards of pasture land, through the little strip of timber which skirted the river bank, and came out on a bar covered with heavy slough grass. At the point of this bar I could see decoys in the water and an unusually high and thick clump of grass which I concluded was a blind, behind which gunners were hidden.

"I walked out quietly, going in from the rear, and was within thirty yards of the blind when three men stood up and faced me. They had dug into the bar so that when they were in a sitting position the grass arranged around the pit hid them completely.

" 'Good morning,' I addressed them as I walked up, and two of the men returned the salutation. 'Gentlemen,' I said, 'I am a United States officer. I wish you would step out of your pit, leaving your guns right where they are.'

"They did as I requested, and I jumped down into their blind and unloaded all three guns. That was a habit.

" 'Now, then,' I said, 'you men are out here breaking the laws of the United States in shooting waterfowl in the spring of the year. What I should do is bundle you up and take you along with me, but if you will show me your state hunting licenses, so that I can identify you later when I need you, I'll let you go on home.'

"Two of the men, the two who had spoken when I approached, promptly produced hunting licenses issued by the state of Kansas. I took out my memorandum book and made a notation of names, addresses and license numbers, and compared the descriptions given on the licenses with the respective owners. Three dead ducks were lying to one side of the blind. All of these I planned to take along as evidence.

"From the looks of things I concluded that the reason I heard no shooting when I first stopped was due to the fact that the gunners had just arrived at the scene of action and were placing their decoys in the water and building their blind.

"Up until this time the third man had not spoken. 'Where's your license?' I asked him, but he did not reply.

"This man, who was apparently either deaf, dumb or both, was a whale of a fellow. About twenty-five years old, he was as perfect a specimen of physical manhood as I ever looked upon. A decided blond, with rosy cheeks, he stood about six foot two and must have weighed 220 pounds, and he looked to be all muscle.

" 'Let me have your license,' I asked him a second time. And still he made no reply.

" 'What's the matter with this fellow?' I asked his companions.

"Neither volunteered any information, so I proceeded to explain to the silent one in detail that unless he could show me a state hunting license or some other means whereby I could identify him when I wanted him later, I would be compelled to take him to Wichita. He stood there with a stolid expression on his face as though he had not heard a word I said.

" 'Is he deaf?' I asked his friends, and one replied, 'No, he ain't deaf.' This was said in a rather surly tone.

" 'Well, then, what ails you?' I asked. 'I'm not a state officer. If you haven't a state hunting license, I do not intend to prosecute you in state courts. You're in bad enough now, breaking the Federal law. What I want is some means of identification. If you haven't a state license, give me some positive proof as to who you are and where you live.'

"He stood and looked at me.

"It was one of the rawest, meanest days that I was ever out. I had been shivering, but now I was getting over it a little. I could feel my temper rising.

" 'My friend,' I said, 'I'm through fooling with you. If you don't produce in short order, back you go to Wichita.'

"When I said this he sat down flat in the snow, with legs spread far apart. 'Take me,' was all he said.

"As I sized up the situation I began to shiver and shake again. This condition may not have been entirely due to the inclement weather; I was up against it. Here was two hundred and twenty pounds of beef and brawn which I had been delegated to transport bodily to a certain automobile some three hundred yards distant. My weight then was about 165 pounds with my hat on. I was up against it —up against it right.

"Here I was, alone with three men, one of them evidently a lunatic. I had an eighteen-year-old boy waiting for me out on the road. He wouldn't have been any help if I had him there. In the back of my mind I felt I could locate this fellow through his friends when I got ready.

But I had made the bluff of taking him to Wichita if he didn't come across.

"Back at the point at the edge of the upland grew a few scattered locust trees. I walked back and, taking my pocket knife, cut one that was about an inch in diameter, and from it I made a nice, handy little club about two feet long. As I stood rounding the ends with my knife the two men who had willingly given me their licenses watched the procedure with much interest.

"The big brute sitting flat on the ground was looking straight ahead of him and apparently was unconcerned about what I was doing. When I finished trimming up my club until it suited me, I walked over in front of him, standing between his feet. I again addressed him.

" 'Now, then, my friend,' I said, 'as I told you, I'm through fooling with you. I'm going to take you to Wichita and turn you over to the United States Marshal to hold for investigation. I'm through fooling. Do you hear me? You're too big a man for me to tackle in your present condition, and I don't intend to lay a hand on you until you're limp. In a very few minutes, if you don't decide to come across clean, I'm going to lay this club right along the side of your left ear. After that I'm going to grab you by the feet and drag you out to the car.'

" 'Give him your license, Harry,' said one of the fellows standing by.

" 'Go ahead, give it to him. Don't be a fool,' said the other man.

"And with that I noticed for the first time the change in Harry's expression. Instead of a look of bulldog determination, fear was visualized in every feature. The pink in his cheeks was disappearing. An ashy gray crept up from the neck of his flannel shirt until his face looked almost like that of a dead man.

" 'Unless you come across quick,' I said to him, 'I'm going to hit you.'

"And with that he turned over on one knee. The man was actually nauseated. I never saw anything like it before or since. He was the sickest fellow I ever saw. And he was fumbling in his pockets looking for something, probably some form of identification. The fellow was whipped.

"He was shaking like a leaf and begging as you never heard a man beg before. 'Please, mister, I've got a hunting license. Don't take me to Wichita. I beg of you! Both these men will tell you who I am and where I live. Please let me go!'

"Both men started to tell me who he was and where he lived, but I told them to be quiet. I was having my innings now.

" 'I'm not interested in what your friends say. I'm talking to you,' I told him. 'Produce something!'

"And with that the poor, miserable fellow came out with a perfectly good Kansas hunting license giving the name of Harry Martin and a small town in the immediate vicinity as his residence. The description on the license fitted him perfectly, but he had made me suffer and I felt, now that I was holding the other end of the rope, I might as well tighten up on it a little.

" 'Who'd you borrow this license from?' I asked him. 'I don't believe it's yours. I think the thing for me to do is to take you to Wichita anyway.'

"Then I listened to more begging and pleading. Both the other men joined in and assured me that this license was authentic; they would guarantee it. I let him suffer for a while to repay me in part for the torture I had been going through. I took down his name, license number and address, and picked up my three ducks, satisfied to be on my way without having to return to the city with a prisoner.

"Two days later I was sitting in the United States Marshal's office in Wichita talking to Deputy Marshal Jim Hill, and I told him about this great big hulk of a fellow who was so yellow that fear of getting hit on the head with a dainty little locust club had caused him to suffer the agonies of six weeks of seasickness in five minutes.

"Hill listened to my yarn, and then he reached over on his desk and picked up one of these contraptions that you file bills on by jabbing them down over an upright ice-pick. He began looking through these slips, and I noticed that each bill started out with the word 'Reward' or the word 'Wanted.' Some offered $50, some offered $500 for knowledge of the whereabouts of the individual whose picture was printed below. Post-office thieves, men escaped from Federal prisons, poor fellows who had tried to get rich quick by the use of Uncle Sam's mails, and other unfortunates were accurately described.

"As the marshal ran through these I saw him hesitate a minute at one and pull it off the peg. 'Is this your bird?'

he asked as he handed it to me, and I read 'One hundred dollars reward for the arrest and conviction of Harry Martin, first-class seaman . . .' "

"That's as far as I read.

" 'You're a fine officer,' remarked Hill, 'to let one hundred smackers slide through your hands as easily as that!' "

IDAHO POTATOES

THE Idaho warden was having his troubles. Somebody was shooting young sage hens. Not only that, but they were shooting them on a game preserve where sage hens were naturally more plentiful than in open shooting territory.

He had put in quite a little time trying to pick up the guilty party, without success. Distances in that country are great, and a man can cover a very limited area where roads are few and far between.

One morning it looked as if luck had dealt him a good hand. A car had backed off the mountain road, right at the edge of the refuge. It was backed in behind a thick clump of aspen and well hidden. A less observant eye than the warden's would not have seen the wheel marks in the road. In fact, he might not have seen them if it hadn't been for the glint of sunlight on the windshield or a bit of nickel which had caught his eye from the other side of the valley.

This probably would be a waiting game, but waiting is hard work, especially when you hear a shotgun pop occasionally back in the game refuge where no shooting is allowed. So the warden backed his car in and placed it in such a way that the other car couldn't be moved until he got his car out first.

Then this protector of Idaho's game took the trail. He

found some empty shells, and when a shell was found he would circle it, making the circle ever larger. By this process he found patches of feathers where sage hens had bumped the ground. He picked up several large wing-feathers and stuck them in his pocket, along with the empty shells, as evidence.

The day wore on, but no sight of his man; so he turned and went back to the car to wait it out. Just before dusk a man came walking down the road without a gun. The warden knew him and accused him of shooting in the refuge. He indignantly denied it, saying that he'd been up into this country looking over some sheep ranges and had parked his car in the refuge simply to get it off the road. He had no gun, and there was nothing the warden could do but let him take his car and go home.

Then a bright idea struck this Idaho game warden. There were probably two of these sage-hen shooters. The other fellow was going down the other side of the mountain with the guns and the game, where he could be picked up later. Getting into his car, the warden raced over those mountain roads in order to be there first. He found some-one waiting, all right, but it was the man's wife and little daughter, with one shotgun—but no game. In due time a neighbor drove up and got the wife and daughter. It was pitch-black by the time he arrived. The warden kept the gun to add to his evidence.

There was no question about this fellow's guilt, but there was a question as to whether or not he could be convicted. The gun was the same gauge as the empty shells. The firing-pin in this gun didn't strike the primer squarely. The empty shells were all punched off-center. Then there were the feathers!

Next morning, the warden searched the mountain to the best of his ability, trying to find the cached game. Under the law, the dead game is *prima facie* evidence. Without it the warden was afraid his case would fail. He had the gun, he had the shells and he had the feathers. If he had one dead sage hen, he could convict. He telephoned his nearest district supervisor and asked him to come over.

When the supervisor heard the story he shook his head. "You'll get beat sure, without some dead game. Better drop it."

The two men were at lunch in the warden's camp.

IDAHO POTATOES

On the table was a dish of giant Idaho baked potatoes.

"I've got an idea," said the warden, "and it may work."

Taking a couple of these potatoes, he wrapped each in a newspaper. Then he took several of the wing-feathers and stuffed them into the fold of the paper so that just the tips stuck out. "Come on," he said to the supervisor, "let's go talk to the guy."

The sage-hen hunter met them with a grin on his face. He was cocky, confident. He either knew the law or he had talked to a lawyer.

"It's going to be much easier for you," said the warden, "if you plead guilty. If we have to go to court with you, your fine is going to be a lot stiffer."

"I haven't shot any sage-hens, and you can go to court whenever you please," said the fellow. "You haven't got any evidence to convict me and you know it, and I don't intend to be talked into admitting I'm guilty when I'm not."

They were standing by the warden's car. "Well," he said, "I guess you know what's best for you," and he opened the door. On the seat lay a pair of binoculars and the two Idaho baked potatoes, and he shoved them over as he was about to get in. The fellow saw them and he saw the sage-hen feathers sticking out of the paper. His Adam's-apple made a couple of trips up and down his neck and his eyes started to climb right out of his head.

"You know," he said between gulps, "maybe you fellows are right. I didn't kill any sage hens, but it looks like the circumstantial evidence is all against me. It would cost me a lot to fight the case, so I guess I'll just pay the fine. What's it goin' to cost me?"

CONTEMPT OF COURT

O<small>NE</small> morning in September my youngest son and I were working out a couple of bird dogs. We were in the fields that lie along Saxon Woods in Westchester

County. A shot rang out from down in the woods. In a few minutes there was another. Song-bird shooters, I thought, and we headed down that way, going quietly with the dogs at heel.

When we reached the point that I thought was pretty close to where the shooting was taking place, we stopped to wait for another shot. The robins were flocking, preparatory to moving south. A number of them flew into a tall beech tree. A shot was fired, and I saw one fall. Under this beech tree we found a well-dressed Italian who spoke perfect English, and he was carrying an expensive Francotte gun. He said he was shooting starlings, which aren't protected, and he had two to prove it. But under the tree we found the robin I'd seen fall and which he hadn't picked up. Even with the help of the bird dogs we could find no other birds.

Then this man yelled something in Italian, and the conclusion was that either another gunner was with him or some companion who carried the game was near-by and had been warned. I placed the man under arrest and went back to my car and circled Saxon Woods in the hope of picking up his companion. We found his parked car. It would have been useless to wait longer; and besides, the man under arrest was demanding that he immediately be taken before the judge, which was his right.

I took him to the nearest police station where he was booked for trial. His gun and the birds were left with the police. Then I telephoned to the State Game Protector to take over from there.

Several nights later the Game Protector told me he wanted me as a witness, that the man wouldn't plead guilty, and that, furthermore, he had hired a whole flock of attorneys and was going to fight the case. There was quite a gathering that evening before the local judge. I talked with the Italian and told him I might withdraw the case and take him before the United States Commissioner and prosecute him under Federal law, for both the state and the Federal laws forbid the shooting of robins.

My whole idea was to scare him into pleading guilty. Instead, he scared me. He talked to his attorneys. They talked to the judge, who threatened to fine me for contempt of court. I never understood just why I was in contempt, but I was very nice about it and didn't argue as the judge laced it into me before those present.

CONTEMPT OF COURT

Apparently I had done a terrible thing. I had insulted the court by intimating that the judge was not competent to try a man for shooting a little bird. That was an unheard-of affront! And to talk about taking such a trivial case before a United States judge was ridiculous!

The judge ranted on and on, and I was very uncomfortable. His knowledge of law was very meager, for he kept repeating that there was no Federal law forbidding the shooting of birds.

"It is absurd," he said, "to think that the great United States courts would stoop to consider the case of a man shooting a little bird in violation of a state game law."

Who was I to argue with him in his own court? I didn't go so far as to agree with him that a Federal court had no jurisdiction in such matters, but I wanted to. I was willing to agree to almost anything. I have the reputation of being noisy when I think I am right. This time I knew I was right, but I was very quiet.

The trial took place. Both sides were heard in detail. After the calling down I had received I felt sure the judge would turn the fellow loose. But he was still the judge, and he found this man guilty and fined him $50. The money apparently had no effect on the song-bird shooter. He paid the fine willingly, and he had plenty more where it came from. Then a look of great distress came over his face, and he turned to me.

"Do I get my gun back?" he asked.

"Sure," I replied. And right then I came nearer being kissed by a man than I have ever been before or since. I'd seen it happen in the movies, but this fellow was so happy that I had to hold him off.

"You're okay, Mr. Warden," he said. "I like you! You are a fine man. We are friends. You like me? Sure! We like each other. We're gooda friends!"

PLUME HUNTERS

WHEN serving as District Inspector in the
United States Bureau of Biological Survey, I received a
letter from Washington telling me to investigate the

plume hunters who were operating on a lake in northern Arkansas near the Mississippi River. The letter went into some detail, giving me the name of a man living on the lake who could be depended upon to help us. The Bureau had been in correspondence with this man about the shooting, and he had told them he had seen evidence of it and would help in any way he could to stop it.

It was a tough place to get to, but a deputy and I finally found our man and, as Washington had assured me, he was more than anxious to cooperate. The next morning he took me in a dugout, and one of his sons took the deputy, and we went out through the cypress swamp to the main lake. The deputy was a big man, and his dugout wasn't wide enough for him to sit down in. He lapped over the sides and, not being used to such a tricky craft, he was afraid even to turn his head. I'm sure he didn't draw a full breath until we got back to shore.

Standing in the stern with a long pole, these men could shoot the hollow cypress logs through the water at a good speed. The trip was worth the discomfort for, although the flesh-eating bugs of all kinds had made that particular swamp their headquarters, wood ducks and hooded mergansers were constantly leaving the water ahead of us; occasional flocks of mallard flushed; the tall cypress trees were filled with herons and anhingas, or snake birds, and cormorants were mixed with the plumaged birds.

When we came to the rookery, we saw as disgusting a spectacle as I have ever witnessed. The water was covered with the bodies of dead herons. The plumes of the American egrets and the snowy herons had been ripped from their breasts and backs, and the carcasses left to rot. Also, the water was strewn with many dead fledglings which had tumbled out of the nests above after the parent birds had been killed, and they had been left to starve. Aigrettes which women wore on their hats were made from egret and other heron feathers. These plumes were at their best during the breeding season, and then was the easiest time to kill the old birds as they came to the nests to feed their young.

Well, we saw the evidence, and that's about all it amounted to. We hung around a couple of days, hoping to hear shooting, but it was plainly evident we were too late and this rookery would probably not be shot again until the next spring.

PLUME HUNTERS

Our host was very co-operative and urged us to stay until we could catch the "dirty plume hunters." His home was our home. He wanted to help. But it wasn't a nice place to spend a vacation. These folks had no screens in the windows. At meal times it was necessary to shoo the flies with one hand while you tried to get food to your mouth with the other. But our host was very hospitable with what he had and very anxious to help the Government in every way he could.

I had left word with the driver of the car who took us in to come back the morning of the third day to see if we wanted to go out. We were both glad when that morning dawned.

Why I decided to go up in the loft of the small shed on the premises I don't know, unless I had done everything else there was to do around the place. I was surprised to find some very nice egret plumes tied in small bunches. There were no skins with the feathers attached, and my host was quick to explain that these were loose feathers he had picked up in the rookery.

"Wouldn't you like to take 'em along with you?" he asked. "Maybe your wife would like 'em."

I took them. It was a violation of the law to possess them. We had all the evidence needed for a conviction.

I made no arrest, maybe because I had had enough of the country and surroundings for the time being. I was ready to go back to civilization. Besides, the man couldn't get away. We could go back and get him any time we wanted him. I never let him know that I had any idea he was guilty of breaking the law.

I made my report to Washington, for there was no question in my mind as to his guilt. I received a reply assuring me that the man was a friend of the Bureau and that he was probably truthful in saying these were just feathers he had picked up.

I chalked it off as another example of the strange workings of the official Washington mind.

THE DYNAMITE DEER

WHEN my boys were growing up, we spent as much time as possible in the Adirondacks during the trout season. Our favorite camping spot was on the east branch of the Ausable between the towns of Keene and Upper Jay. We had a tent with just enough floor space to accommodate a double air mattress and three single bed rolls for the three sons. The boys built a rock fireplace in front of the tent, and we did our eating under a fly. Breakfast was the only meal we took at home. From this point we radiated out to all the good trout waters in the vicinity, and we ate our lunches and dinners in villages as near our pet fishing spots as possible.

For a number of years we used this camp site for ten days or two weeks twice each season. It was ideal. From the main highway we crossed the Ausable on an old iron bridge into a big meadow; then, turning south, we drove down through the meadow for a couple of hundred yards to the bank of the stream, which at this point was a hundred yards away from the highway.

Right behind our tent was a good pool. There was another excellent pool where the stream turned west from the highway, and from that point on up to the iron bridge was good fishing water. So it wasn't always necessary to take the car to some remote spot if one of us wanted to fish while the others loafed in the middle of the day.

THE DYNAMITE DEER

Now, it so happens that, once a game warden, always a game warden. Any man who has sincerely worked for the protection of game and fish doesn't get over it. I don't mean that such a fellow has to be officiously checking up on everyone he meets afield, making arrests for technical and minor violations and otherwise making himself a nuisance, but when he learns of a really vicious violation the chances are that he will go into action.

For a number of years the Hollands had patronized every eating place along the East and West Branches of the Ausable, the Bouquet and other trout streams lying on the eastern slopes of the Adirondacks. We made friends with these folks and often had a good fish to give away. One evening a restaurant keeper took me aside.

"Don't get me mixed up in this thing," he said, "but some fellows from Ausable Forks are going to shoot a couple of holes in the river Saturday night. They are aiming to shoot that big pool at the bend of the river near your camp. I thought you'd like to know it."

The next day was Friday; so I drove to Lake Placid to see the local New York State game protector. Most of the telephones in that section were on party lines, and it would have been a mistake to trust information of that kind to the general public. I told the protector that I knew the lay of the land and would help, and suggested that he not show himself along the East Branch in daylight, but instead come to my camp after dark Saturday night.

I never knew for sure whether this game protector had mental reservations against approaching these fellows in the dark or whether they were friends of his. Dynamiting is a felony, and men who will dynamite fish might prefer to shoot an ordinary game protector rather than run the risk of becoming a boarder in the State Penitentiary. Instead of following our plan as decided upon, this game protector telephoned the game protector in Elizabethtown, who appeared in Keene Saturday afternoon in full uniform, where he was met by the protector from Lake Placid, also dressed as New York State adorns her wardens. They held a consultation, and the rumor even reached *us* that dynamiters were planning to shoot the river and that the game protectors were going to stop it. They did! That night was just as peaceful as any other night along the Ausable.

THE DYNAMITE DEER

Several nights later I was lying in the tent half asleep when a car rumbled across the iron bridge and turned south into our meadow. The headlights hit straight on the door of our tent. The car stopped and the lights were switched off.

"There they are," I said to myself, "and it's up to me to be there when they dynamite the pool."

I got into some clothes and took a 12-gauge pumpgun, eased a shell into the chamber and filled the magazine. It was about as dark as a night ever gets. To the west of our meadow lay a mountain. I figured that perhaps the best and safest plan was to sneak up alongside the mountain to the dirt road which ran from the main highway across the bridge and up into the hills. I could then follow the road back to the river and either wait at the car for the dynamiters to return with the fish or at least be between them and their car. If I got my courage up to the proper point, I might even carry out my first plan of being right at the pool when they shot it.

Sure, I was scared. I've been scared lots of times. The more I thought about the job I'd taken on, the surer I was that this was a foolhardy venture. There were probably three or four of them, and things might not work out as I had planned.

It was chilly, and the high weeds and grass along the mountain were wet with dew. Maybe that's why I shivered. About half-way from our camp to the road was an acre or so of truck garden belonging to a man who lived across the main highway. He had a dandy garden—sweet corn, beans, peas, Swiss chard and a number of other vegetables. There was a good breeze blowing from the north. I reached this garden patch and was thankful for the path between it and the mountain, where I could walk without wading through the dripping grass.

Most outdoor men have heard a buck deer's whistle. It's an impressive sound, especially if the deer is close to you. On this particular night there was a buck deer in that garden patch, helping himself. The wind gave him no warning that I was coming. I must have almost stepped on him, and when he snorted it sounded as loud to me as a main-line express train screaming for a crossing. I was ready to be scared, and I am frank to say I never have been scared worse. I don't know why I didn't shoot a couple of times at something. Incidentally, I knew what had happened, but it didn't help any. I had an almost uncontrollable desire to sit down.

I don't know how many minutes I stood there, but it was a long time before I got up courage enough to continue on to the road. While I waited, trying to get myself together, I couldn't help but consider the evidence if one of my friends on the State force had been in that car and flashed his headlights my way. There I stood, with a fully loaded gun, apparently trying to kill a deer to get a little summer mutton.

Sure, I finally got nerve enough to continue on my way. I located the car and eased up to it, still jumpy. The lights were out, and everything was quiet. All I would have to do was wait until the dynamiters returned. Then I heard a girl's voice say, "Jim, we must go home!" Just a man and a girl in a parked automobile, telling each other sweet nothings!

Coachwhip Publications

CoachwhipBooks.com

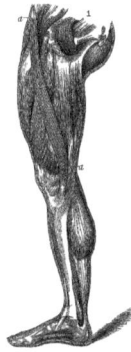

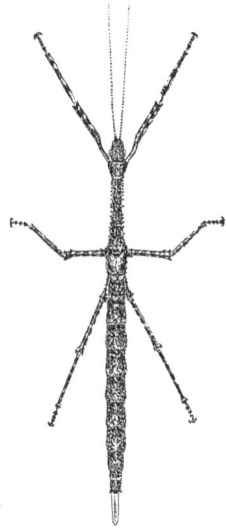

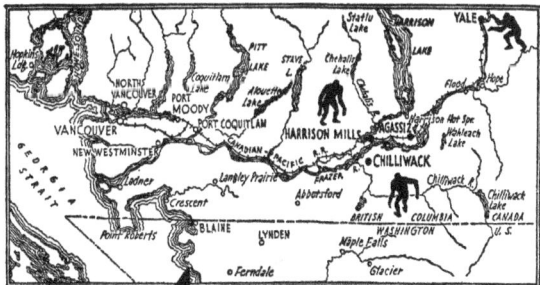

COACHWHIP PUBLICATIONS

COACHWHIPBOOKS.COM

VARMINTS

CHAD ARMENT

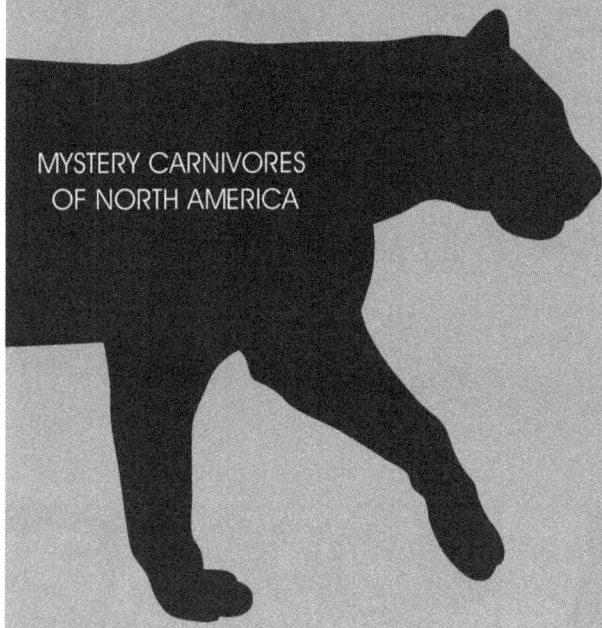

MYSTERY CARNIVORES
OF NORTH AMERICA

An extensive catalogue of sightings and
stories of black panthers and other carnivorous
mystery animals in North America.

COACHWHIP PUBLICATIONS

COACHWHIPBOOKS.COM

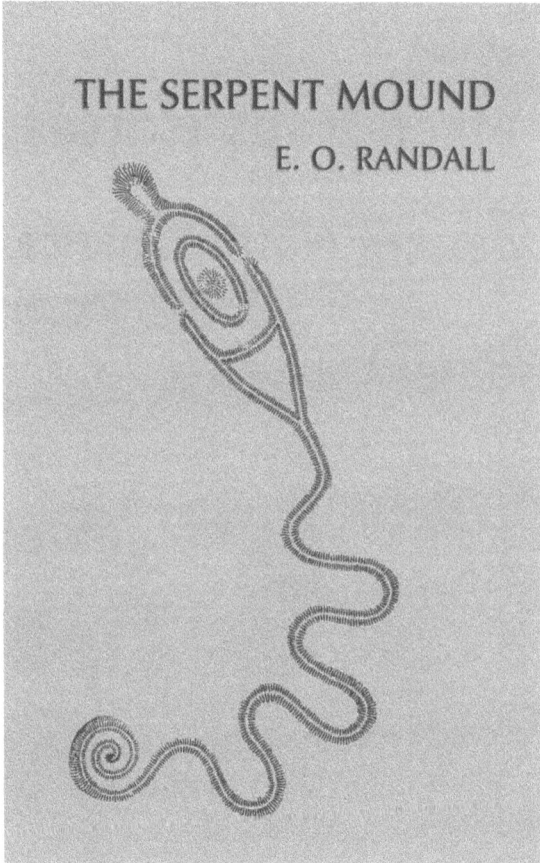

THE SERPENT MOUND

E. O. RANDALL

Reprint of an early classic description
of the Great Serpent Mound of
Adams County, Ohio.

COACHWHIP PUBLICATIONS

COACHWHIPBOOKS.COM

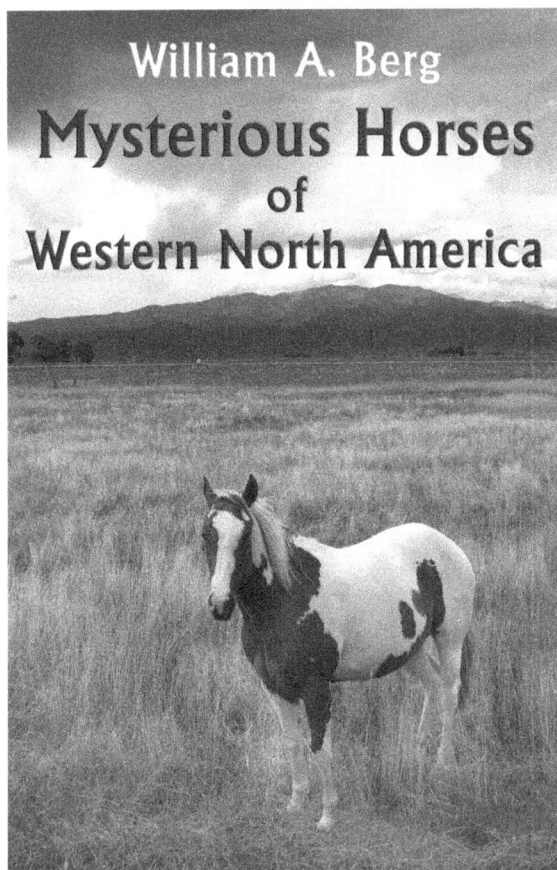

William A. Berg

Mysterious Horses
of
Western North America

A fascinating historical discussion of
the origin of the Paint and Appaloosa
horses of the Wild West.

COACHWHIP PUBLICATIONS

COACHWHIPBOOKS.COM

PRIMITIVE AND PIONEER SPORTS

FOR RECREATION TODAY

Bernard S. Mason

How to have fun with the "toys" of yesteryear:
lariets, tomahawks, whips, and more.

www.ingramcontent.com/pod-product-compliance
Lightning Source LLC
LaVergne TN
LVHW091221080426
835509LV00009B/1102